The
Nine Lives
of a
Fighter Pilot

The Nine Lives of a Fighter Pilot

Terence Kelly

Airlife

By the same author

Non-fiction
Hurricane Over the Jungle
Hurricane and Spitfire Pilots at War

Battle for Palembang

Plays
A Share in the Sun
  (with Campbell Singer)
Just Before Dawn (from Elleston
  Trevor's – A Place for the Wicked)
Carnival in Trinidad
The Masterminds

Divorce in Chancery
Four Sided Triangle
The Genki Boys
Honest Tom
Stella

Novels
Properjohn
The Developers
The Blades of Cordoba
Revolution on St Barbara
Voyage Beyond Belief

The Carib Sands
The Genki Boys
Play in a Hot Summer
Fepow

Copyright © 2003 Terence Kelly

First published in the UK in 2003
by Airlife Publishing Ltd

British Cataloguing-in-Publication Data
  A catalogue record for this book
  is available from the British Library

ISBN 1 84037 390 3

Typeset by Phoenix Typesetting, Burley-in-Wharfedale, West Yorkshire
Printed in England by Biddles Ltd,. www.biddles.co.uk

*Contact us for a free catalogue that describes the complete range of Airlife books for pilots and
aviation enthusiasts.*

Airlife Publishing Ltd
101 Longden Road, Shrewsbury, SY3 9EB, England
E-mail: sales@airlifebooks.com
Website: www.airlifebooks.com

PREFACE

WHEN Terence Kelly asked me to write the preface to this book I felt honoured, but also doubtful of my qualifications to do so. Over the years I have come to respect him as one of the toughest and most resilient men I have ever met. As his book demonstrates so evocatively, he was a wartime Hurricane pilot who had a very adventurous time flying operationally before suffering all the horrific life-threatening ill-treatment and indignities inflicted upon him as a Japanese prisoner of war for nearly three and a half years. My own 'under fire' experiences during the Second World War, on the other hand, were limited to those of a schoolboy subjected to the Liverpool blitz in 1941. Moreover, although I was accepted at the age of seventeen for aircrew training by the Royal Air Force in 1944, for various reasons I did not reach my first operational squadron until 1948.

In mitigation of my presumption in undertaking this task I should say that the squadron concerned was at the time equipped with Spitfires; that the flying training I had was of a standard very similar to Terence's; and that my subsequent flying included most of the fighters operated by the RAF between then and the late seventies, culminating with Lightnings and Phantoms. Whilst I did not have anything to compare with Terence's Second World War operational experience I believe that I can empathise very closely with the feelings invoked in several of the 'lives' in this wonderfully eclectic selection.

In my early flying days I, too, was euphemistically 'uncertain of my position' on several occasions and had to rely on combinations of luck plus only barely formed flying skills to retrieve the situation. I, too, remember not a little apprehension before my first night solo flight, albeit in my case in a Tiger Moth rather than a Master but, somewhat coincidentally, also from a Scottish airfield surrounded by hills. In neither case, however, did I have such hair-raising experiences as are so graphically described in the first two chapters of this book. On the other hand, shortly after completing my training I had a very similar experience to that of Terence when, whilst venturing to do some cloud-flying in a Spitfire, I found myself in the same sort of terrifying spiral dive as he did. In my case it only came right when I broke out of the bottom of the cloud to find a bare few hundred feet to spare above the mountains below.

Wartime pilot training was necessarily concerned with turning out large numbers of operational pilots and, whilst generally effective in that imperative, it reached nothing like the standard enjoyed by Royal Air Force trainees today. This was particularly true of instrument flying instruction, a problem that only really started to be addressed intensively in the mid-fifties, and which must certainly have contributed to the number of wartime and immediate post-war flying accidents. Terence Kelly muses in one of his early chapters about the number of deaths caused by flying accidents compared with those brought about by enemy action. I have no knowledge of these figures, but I do remember being told at a post-war flight safety seminar that during the Second World War more RAF aircraft were involved in accidents than were destroyed by the enemy.

This book is the condensed wartime history of a remarkable man. It will appeal to all who like their adventure stories based on fact; to all those who are fascinated with the thoughts that drove the Second World War fighter pilot; to all who have themselves been privileged to fly operational fighter aircraft; and to all those who believe it is necessary to keep in the public mind the appalling treatment inflicted by the Japanese upon their prisoners of war.

Air Vice-Marshal
N. S. Howlett CB
Lower Shiplake
Oxon
January 2002

CONTENTS

Black on Black and Steer on the Lubber Line

THE civilian called to serve with the RAF as a would-be pilot presented himself at a Receiving Wing (in my case No. 1, Receiving Wing, Babbacombe, Devon) and here he spent two weeks being inoculated against all manner of diseases, being kitted out with his uniform and, with a certain amount of drilling and the like, being introduced to service life.

From his Receiving Wing he was posted to an Initial Training Wing (ITW), my own being No. 2 ITW at Cambridge. He would reckon to spend some seven or so weeks here, the time being spent in concentrated drilling and PT and in learning certain martial arts such as Radio Telegraphy, the Morse Code, map reading and plotting, how to strip down a rifle into its component parts and reassemble it, and suchlike exercises. I do not recall that (except possibly the map reading) any of these set tasks were of the slightest use in the future, but had I failed my flying tests presumably they might have been, in some other branch of the service into which I would have been directed.

At Cambridge I was one of twenty or so billeted in one of the colleges, Trinity Hall, where quite a number of undergraduates were still in residence. So far as I remember we held the lowest RAF rank – that of AC2 – (Aircraftsman Second Class) and I believe our pay was 2/- (10p) a day. We were, however, distinct from all other RAF uncommissioned personnel in that in our forage cap peaks we wore a piece of white material – known as a white flash – which distinguished us from the *hoi polloi* and of which we were immensely proud.

At the end of the course we were posted to one of the several Elementary Flying Training Schools (EFTS), mine being No. 5 EFTS Meir, near Stoke-on-Trent. On arrival we were directed to the Town Hall, where we spent the first night sleeping on its floor. Had it not been that our date of arrival is recorded in my Log Book as 14 September 1940, I would have guessed it as the fifteenth for I recall very clearly listening to a radio announcement that the RAF had shot down the largest number of German aircraft destroyed in a single day and I remember that our glee was watered down by the reflection that if the chaps who were already flying their Hurricanes and Spitfires went on like this much longer there wouldn't be any Dorniers, Heinkels or Messerschmitts left for us.

Without much ado we began our flying training. So far as I know and believe at this stage in the war the majority of stations used Tiger Moths for elementary flying training but at Meir we had Miles Magister monoplanes. This is something I have always regretted. There was nothing the matter with the Magister, which was a benign and friendly aircraft, but the biplane Tiger Moth, with its struts and wires and above all, its history, had a romance about it which the Magister quite lacked. The only times I was to know the joy of flying a Tiger Moth were when I went on occasional London leaves from one or other of the stations to which I had by then been posted.

At Meir we were taught the basics of flying aircraft: taxying, taking off and landing, straight and level flying, climbing, gliding and stalling, medium and steep turns, spinning and recovering from spins, instrument flying, precautionary and forced landings, sideslipping, aerobatics, low flying and such exotic exercises as stopping and restarting an engine during flight, and how to abandon an aircraft *in extremis*. Apart from those who failed the Flight Commander's Test we each did about fifty hours' flying of which, very approximately, half was dual and half was solo. The course lasted through six very pleasant weeks and so far as I recall was without important incident. If there were accidents they must have been minor ones and certainly no one was killed, nor even, so far as I know, injured. At our next station, Montrose, it was to be another matter.

Montrose is in County Angus, Scotland, and lies approximately halfway between Dundee to the south and Aberdeen to the north. I understand that nowadays a golf course occupies the territory on which No. 8 Flying Training Station (FTS) Montrose was based.

The airfield ran roughly south-west to north-east and had been created out of the narrowish plain, perhaps four or so miles wide, between on the one side the North Sea and on the other the Grampian Mountains. At its southern extremity lies the small town of Montrose squeezed between the sea and the Montrose Basin, which is a remarkable stretch of water approximately two miles square which is connected to the ocean by a narrow channel. At the northern extremity of the airfield were wind-blown sandhills up to (memory tells me) about 150 feet in height.

The winter of 1940/41 was very cold, and snow which fell in November had scarcely thawed on the low ground before it was reinforced by further falls through the later months, whilst the Grampian Mountains, threateningly close and rising to some three thousand feet or more, were largely snowbound through the winter. In the lowland there were many days of rain and snow, or lowering clouds at best, while such sparkling sunlit days as did occur from time to time presented the threat of haar – the cold sea fog which appears dramatically out of a clear blue sky, blotting out the sun in seconds and obliterating the land from the eyes of a circling pilot.

Even these days, for all the state-of-the-art equipment built into modern aircraft, bad weather causes problems, but these are as nothing compared with those it could pose to young, green pilots flying machines which were quite lacking any form of equipment that gave them radio contact with the ground. Moreover, the Master itself greatly augmented these risks. There were at the time basically two types of training aircraft used on Flying Training Stations: the Harvard and the Master. The Harvard was an American animal which, with its radial engine, was outlandishly noisy – but it was a sound machine which, I have heard, lacked nasty habits. Not so the Master. The Master was a low-wing monoplane powered by a Kestrel in-line engine with gull-like wings of considerable dihedral, an aircraft which if pushed even only a trifle beyond the laid-down limits was totally unforgiving.

As may be judged from the above, what with one thing and another No. 8 FTS Montrose was hardly an ideal station at which to train fledgling pilots, especially in winter, and it is perhaps not surprising that through the six winter months while I was there, about ten per cent of those under training were killed through flying accidents. Indeed, it was a rare man who, by the time he passed the Flight Commander's Test and was posted off to his Operational Training Unit (OTU), did not have a least one escape from disaster to shoot his line about.

My own first escape came about in a quite accidental manner. One was presented with a 'sequence of instructions' which had to be pasted into one's Log Book and listed no less than twenty-three items from taxying, through taking off and landing, spinning, aerobatics and so on which had to be performed and, once executed, noted in the Log Book after every flight.

One day, having taken off to perform one or other of these operations, I climbed through a gap in thin low cloud and found myself flying in a fascinating, almost ethereal ambience. Below me, apart from the gap, the cloud stretched levelly in all directions as far as the eye could see; a thousand or so feet above me was an endless, parallel sheet

3

of cloud. Once I had left behind the gap through which I'd climbed and the ground below was no longer visible, I was in a strange, grey, vast but empty cavern-like universe of which I was the sole inhabitant. I flew this way and that, turning, banking and trying one or two manoeuvres before deciding that this was an ideal opportunity to *get some time in* for item number 19 (instrument flying) and practise for the first time flying solo through cloud. I was not enthusiastic to do so but encouraged myself with the reflection that if I got into any difficulties all I needed to do was descend into the empty space below and thence, if my hole was no longer available, fly through the thin lower cloud layer and return to the airfield.

So, somewhat gingerly – for this was a new departure – I pulled up the Master's nose and climbed into the murk above and immediately, and for the first time in my life, I was flying solo in thick fog. It struck me as anything but an enjoyable business but conscience insisted I persist, and so for a few minutes, eyes glued to instruments, I climbed a little and turned a little, lost a little height and climbed again – all this being done very circumspectly.

To the inexperienced, flying in cloud is a disorientating experience. I soon discovered that any preconceived notion that there is some plumb bob built into the body's mechanism which will advise you if you are not flying straight and level is quite wrong: that you are simply in a never-never land of grey in which you have not the slightest idea which way is up, which way is down or even which way is sideways. With as your sole companions the sound of the aircraft's engine and a batch of instruments, you feel astonishingly alone. There is frankly not much fun in it.

And so, conscience satisfied, after perhaps ten unenjoyable minutes I decided to return to the real world. Lowering the Master's nose, I began gently to descend.

In the centre of the main instrument panel there was an artificial horizon (which, for the uninitiated, is an instrument showing a tiny mock-up aircraft which tilts this way or that, and up or down, paralleling the attitude of the aircraft being flown), and all I had to do to get down into the clear air space, somewhere below, was keep this mock-up aircraft in a level plane in a position just below the artificial horizon which paralleled the real horizon I could not see. Directly below the artificial horizon there was a gyro-compass (which, if properly set before take-off, informs a pilot in which magnetic direction he is heading). There is an altimeter (which tells the pilot his height at any given moment and thus whether he is gaining or losing altitude) and an airspeed indicator, which tells him how fast he is flying. There are two additional instruments: the turn-and-bank indicator and the rate-of-climb indicator, but for my purposes the first four mentioned were sufficient. All I had to do was return to the space of clear air between the upper and lower levels of cloud and hopefully rediscover the gap in it through which I had climbed.

Whether or not I had travelled farther than I'd imagined, or, through some vagary of weather the clear air space between the original two layers of cloud had filled in, I shall never know. What I knew at the time was that my altimeter was soon warning me that, bearing in mind the Grampians were somewhere close at hand, while still in cloud I was getting dangerously low. If I continued in this fashion there was every prospect that at any moment, too late to do anything about it, too late even to say a prayer, I would discern through the murk the hillside which was about to put an end not just to my flying career but to myself.

Now the sensible thing would have been to at once turn onto an easterly course and thus make sure the mountains were well behind me but once the fear of crashing into a hillside had seized my mind, the murk seemed horribly full of unpleasant possibilities and I decided instead that the immediate thing to do was to climb high enough to avoid this risk.

But I was by now uneasy, uncertain if the gyro-compass had been properly set before take-off and not at all sure of my ability, while coping with climbing through fog, to fly by the complex P.6 compass with which all Masters were fitted, or even how to use it correctly. A curious incomplete phrase started running through my mind: 'Put-black on black and steer on the lubber line.' But even as I mouthed these words, I knew I hadn't got them correctly. One of the things I was sure about was that you did put black on black and I knew that somewhere on the compass there was a lubber line which came into play, but either because I hadn't done my homework properly – which was unlikely – or because I was by now in a very nervous state, my mind refused to solve the problem. So I decided that the sensible thing to do was to fly up to five thousand feet where there wouldn't be any risk of colliding with a mountain before addling my mind in trying to solve the riddle.

However, having reached five thousand feet, I noticed with considerable relief that there was a faint lightening in the sky above me and a simple solution to my problems occurred to me: I would continue climbing until above the cloud level. Once in clear air I would be able to take a breather and at the same time, by the position of the sun assess reasonably accurately which way was eastwards, check and if necessary adjust my gyro-compass, fly eastwards for long enough to be sure I was over the sea, descend and, having broken cloud, fly westwards until the Scottish coast came in sight and hopefully find the airfield.

Had I been more experienced I would have known that the lightening of a cloud layer can be misleading. Uninitiated, I imagined that if I climbed another thousand feet or so I would be in clear air. But not a bit of it. I climbed – I will not say steadily, for by now uncertain, on edge and totally inexperienced in this sort of junketing, I was continually grossly over-correcting the controls as, with my eyes glued to instruments, I climbed through the formless murk with my altimeter crawling remorselessly round the dial, reading six thousand, seven thousand, eight thousand, nine thousand feet and still the cloud above, although steadily yellowing, obstinately refusing to disperse. To my dismay I saw ice particles forming on the windscreen, then forming and thickening on the leading edges of the mainplanes. Now I was torn by indecision: should I press grimly on, risking the Master becoming unmanoeuvrable through an excess of ice or should I try to set a course eastwards by the P.6 compass? But here I was faced with the same difficulty as before: how to fly by compass had clean gone out of my head. As I struggled to be calm and remember the simple phrase I had been taught, only the words 'put black on black' and 'lubber line' hammered irritatingly and irremovably in my brain. I glared at the instrument – but doing so told me nothing. So far as the use of magnetic compasses was concerned, my mind had become a blank. So there was nothing for it but to press on. And at last with my machine thick and cumbersome with ice, my nerves in tatters, wondering at what height one needed oxygen, I broke cloud!

What a glorious moment that was! I hadn't the least idea where I was, whether over land or sea or whether north or south of Montrose, but above, the sun poured down out of a pure blue sky while below, the clouds, white and glittering, stretched endlessly in all directions.

I forgot the terrible sense of loneliness which had oppressed me on my muddled upwards flight and, for the first time in my life, discovered the serenity and simple beauty of a world above the clouds. With relief pouring into me like air into the lungs of a man who has stretched himself to the limit underwater, I looked about me entranced and filled with joy. And as I looked I saw the ice crystals on the windscreen crumbling and, blown by the slipstream, clearing, and the ice on the mainplanes breaking into lumps and whirling away.

Taking my direction from the sun, I turned roughly eastwards and as my shattered nerves began to settle and the last of the ice was swept away I was conscious of an extraordinary temptation to put from my mind what I still had to do and just fly and fly and fly.

However, having satisfied myself at last that by now I must be over sea I checked my gyro-compass, and with some concern, my petrol gauge, and regretfully I pushed the control column forward. Like a man who, having crossed through a boggy waste, has now to make his way back through it, I re-entered the murk.

Going down again was even worse than coming up, for now I knew what lay ahead: the re-formation of ice on windscreen and wings, and about two miles of the nothingness of directionless cloud between me and safety. And at the back of my mind the question: at the end of it when, hopefully, I broke cloud and emerged into clear air over sea and turned back towards the land, which way would I have to turn when I hit the coast? North or south?

It *was* worse going down, worse and endless. The ice formed and thickened, and far from encouraging by lightening, the fog darkened with every minute. My nerves, already stretched, became ragged. Imagination started to play its part I began to see obstacles looming up ahead of me which could not possibly exist. Over-correcting, through some crass flying error, I toppled the gyro-compass I had so carefully checked and made sure was, for my purposes at least, correct enough. And if this was not bad enough, what was worse still was that once again I toppled the artificial horizon.

Now – a tyro in this sort of exercise – all I had left to help me keep the Master in a level downward path were three remaining instruments: the turn-and-bank to keep me on a straight rather than on a serpentine downward path; the airspeed indicator to make sure I was not either diving too fast or at risk of stall; the altimeter to see how far down I still had to go. And all around me – nothing! Fog, thick, ever-darkening fog. Luck must have indeed been with me. How in some wild over-correction I did not put the Master into a spin, I cannot imagine. There was nothing of the cool, self-assured would-be fighter pilot about me on that cold, drear December day. I was nothing but a sprog, a twenty-year-old, hugely inexperienced and very frightened boy, out of his element, ham-fisted, disbelieving. And dreadfully alone.

I broke cloud at a mere two hundred feet. Below was the cold, grey, wind-tossed North Sea. Of all things I saw a ship – a small freighter or a fishing boat, perhaps. They must have wondered on that ship what on earth a training aircraft (for as we were painted yellow they must have recognised me for what I was), was doing emerging out of cloud so far from land. They could have told me which way to go – had I the means of asking them. I didn't want to lose that ship; its presence was strangely comforting. But the great difference between flying an aircraft and driving a car is that in an aeroplane you cannot stop to ask the way. Nor can you be sure of the road ahead and that before long you will come upon a petrol filling station! Above all you cannot pull into the side of the road to rest a tortured mind. You have no choice but to carry on flying knowing that vital seconds are ticking by and your petrol is running out.

And so all too soon the ship was lost from sight and the same damn phrase was tormenting me. 'Black on black and steer on the lubber line.' Was that what it was? And if it was, what was the lubber line anyway? I tried to thrust it away from me, accepting that if I'd ever known what the phrase meant, I'd forgotten now and that if the answer how to use that blessed compass correctly was stored in my brain, my brain was too disturbed to download it for me.

I concentrated on the compass down there between my knees, watched the wobbling needle. If it pointed that way, that way must be North, I told myself unconvincingly. So, that being so, if it *was* so, what I must do was turn so that in relation to the direction in which I was heading the needle would be pointing to my right. Then I would be flying westward. It seemed so obvious and so simple it was difficult to believe it could be so.

So I was anything but sure whether I was right in this assumption, but with no alternative presenting itself I turned and flew on the resultant course. Squeezed between an angry, wave-tossed, cold, grey sea close below and sullen, threatening rain-charged clouds close above, I flew on and on with nothing changing, with nothing to hint I had not made some crass miscalculation and was heading in the opposite direction to the one I should be taking. And after a while I began to believe this was so, and then to be sure it was. The temptation to turn and fly on a reciprocal course grew strongly, but on checking the fuel gauge I doubted I had sufficient petrol left to go back as far as the point from which I'd started, and then beyond into the unknown distance. I'd have to believe I'd guessed right. It was my only hope.

Guessed right I had. When I had all but abandoned hope, had begun to face up to the ghastly thought of ending up in that icy sea with only my Mae West to keep me company, and begun to consider the alternatives of crash-landing amongst the waves or climbing into the murk and then baling out, I saw a faint line drawn on the horizon, a line so faint and low I thought at first it was a mirage. But with each moment the line thickened and soon I knew I must be looking at the coast of Scotland. When I reached it, there was one thing left to do. To make a guess. Did I turn left? Did I turn right? I guessed left – and my guess was the correct one. I flew close by the shoreline and after a while I found Montrose. I landed without incident and told no one of my experience – to have done so would have been to admit gross incompetence, and one had one's pride.

Only Birds and Fools

As I have written earlier, while I was at Montrose approximately ten per cent of pupils being trained were killed in flying accidents. I write this not merely from recollection but also based on evidence in my Log Book, from which I see that on 17 January 1941 I wrote '5 of 27 course killed' – and the courses consisted of, so far as I remember, about fifty pupils.

The majority of deaths occurred through unauthorised low flying or through night-flying accidents. There was an old RAF saying: 'Only birds and fools fly – and birds don't fly at night', and in our day, when our training aircraft lacked radio communication with the ground, and because of the exigencies of wartime, airfields were so blacked-out as to be quite invisible from above, the saying was felt to have a great deal of truth in it – indeed it was because so many were killed night-flying that the saying came into existence.

In our case its strength as a maxim was underlined by the fact that with our night-flying largely limited to circuits and landings, accidents when they occurred were usually in close proximity to the station. I remember only too well, while playing cards a night or two before I did my first night-flying, hearing a muffled thump and knowing (as did the other card players) exactly what that meant because we had all heard it before, putting down our cards and going outside to stare, sickened, at a ball of yellow flame at the north end of the airfield and wondering who it was who had killed himself this time. While at Montrose I went to more than one funeral, but whether or not I attended the interment of the remains in this case, I do not remember.

As may be imagined there was little enthusiasm to do our night-flying stint and we all crossed our fingers and hoped that when our personal call came it would be on a moonlit night.

I was not to be lucky.

So far as I remember, generally speaking, the system was to get through the night-flying syllabus course by course, by which I mean that one course would complete its syllabus before the next course started on it. Naturally this meant that when one course was nearing its end – when most of its members had done their stint – its numbers were made up by members from the course following.

I cannot anywhere discover the number of my course but with the notification in my Log Book that five of twenty-seven course had been killed, it could have been twenty-eight but was probably (as I shall assume) twenty-six.

It so happened that I was one of the first – if not the very first – to be tagged onto the end of twenty-five course. How they selected which of us it should be I have no idea – most likely by lot, I imagine, for I had shown no particular prowess in my flying. At Meir I had needed more than fourteen hours' dual before being allowed to go solo, and fourteen was quite a few hours more than most of the course had needed, and the notification in my Log Book by the Station Commander at the end of my course at Montrose read simply: 'Average.'

It is quite impossible for me to forget *most* of the events of that night of 28 December 1940 yet curiously all I can remember of the dual instruction I received was my instructor, one Flight Lieutenant Mackenzie, asking me after we had done five circuits and landings if I felt all right for going solo. I felt anything but all right. It was a pitch black, utterly moonless night and the thought of having to venture into it alone filled me with dread. But what could one do but say: 'Yes, Sir.' Which I did.

The experience began with my being taken over to the dispersal hut in a Commer van and the only welcome I got when entering the hut was: 'Shut that bloody door!', which I did willingly enough, for as well as being pitch-black it was bitterly cold outside.

'You're Kelly?'

I turned towards the duty officer who sat behind the only piece of furniture – an old kitchen table with a telephone on it.

'Yes, Sir.'

'Okay.' The duty officer did something with a pen or pencil. 'Find yourself a pew and try and get a bit of sleep. You're not going to be wanted for quite a while.'

I looked round the hut for other members of my course, but I couldn't see any, although I did recognise a few of the course preceding ours. It wasn't really a hut, more a huge overblown packing case with a door at one end of it. There wasn't a window – a window would have presented an extra blackout problem – and the air was hazed with tobacco smoke which smarted the eyes abominably. There were so many pupils in flying kit sprawled about, sitting in small

11

groups chatting or, the lucky ones who'd got there early, lying down using their parachutes as pillows, that at first I couldn't see an empty space anywhere. But eventually I found one. Lumbered with my parachute and impeded by my still-stiff flying boots, it wasn't easy stepping over recumbent bodies to get to it. 'Looks like a bloody battlefield, doesn't it? Join the Raf and find yourself in Calcutta!' was the only sympathy I got, and this from someone I didn't know. I agreed it did and busied myself extracting, with considerable difficulty, my cigarette case out of an inner pocket. I was contemplating the wisdom of offering one to the pupil who'd spoken to me when the telephone abruptly rang. The effect was remarkable. Conversation ceased and except for heads turning towards the duty officer, the hut was of a sudden filled with statues, upraised hands held motionless cigarettes, a man shifting his position to be more comfortable remained bent over, stiff as a ramrod, knee on floor.

The duty officer answered crisply: 'Right!', put the phone back on the hook, and glancing at his list, called out a name. From out of the welter of bodies a pupil extracted himself and with great difficulty, encumbered by gear, staggered rather than stepped over those between him and the door, placing his feet carefully in such spaces as he could find for them. At the door, where there was more room because it was the coldest place, he put on his helmet, fixed his goggles, slid his hands into silk undergloves, woollen gloves and gauntlets, lifted the parachute he'd allowed to slip to the floor and with it swinging clumsily behind him, blundered out. One or two 'good lucks' drifted after him into the night.

I lit my cigarette, put the case away and secretly started counting, then did arithmetic and taking into account the dual circuits and bumps some probably had still to do with an instructor before going solo, I figured it was very unlikely they'd get round to me tonight and I wondered why I'd been sent over at all when there were all these chaps from the course ahead of me still to do their stint.

The snarl of an engine cut across my thoughts and stifled such desultory conversation as had restarted. Thin blue threads of smoke climbed straight to the blackened ceiling. Only the duty officer, scrawling something in his notebook, was pretending not to listen, pretending not to have been affected by the fact that other men he'd sent out previously had killed themselves – had ended up drowned or killed outright in the Montrose Basin or in a ball of yellow flame beyond the sand dunes at the north end of the airfield, as Garland (or whatever the man's name had been) had done.

The engine note became a roar and the hut shivered a trifle from its vibration. The sound began to fade into a hum and as it did conversation restarted, louder than before, more forced. Why don't we just say it, I thought? Why don't we shout it out? 'Freeman' – another name I've selected at random – 'Freeman's unstuck, lucky bugger! Now all he's got to do is get the bloody thing down again!'

A couple of hours passed. Freeman had done his dual circuits and landings. So had Wakeman and Glyn-Davies or whatever their names were. It struck me there was no sense to it – it wasn't even alphabetical. But at least there was enough room now to stretch out using the parachute pack as a pillow. They were hard and the curve of them held your head up at an unnatural angle. So they weren't very comfortable; but they were comforting. To my surprise I was feeling drowsy. But it was warm in the hut, the double blackout door kept the winter out. You would never have known there were still patches of snow outside or that the Grampians were covered. It had been a hard winter. For a time the airfield had been deep in snow and the Commanding Officer had conceived the brilliant idea of having the entire station's complement, every man-jack of it, and all the Waafs, lined up at one end of the airfield and then he had led the way two paces ahead, his great-coat flapping in the bitter wind, like a Russian general leading the Reds, or maybe the Whites, in a march across the steppes against the enemy. He'd looked impressive, the CO, swashbuckling, leading the long, straggling line of hundreds of men and women in Air Force blue marching through the snow. It had been like something in a film. But when we got to the end and turned round to see what we had done it had been a let-down. Almost funny! For instead of the snow being flattened enough for us to restart flying, there was nothing but a few footprints in it!

Well, thank God, I mused, most of the snow at the lower levels had melted in that brief milder spell, but the wind was from the north-east again and outside it was cold enough to freeze the balls off a brass monkey. You had to search for places to be really warm. Like this one was! Or had been – when the hut had been packed to bursting. It was colder now. By the time it was my turn to fly – if my turn came tonight, which I doubted – doubted hopefully – it'd probably be freezing. But it'd still be warm in the aircrew mess. The lucky blighters who were fireproof because they'd done their night solos on moonlit nights would be sitting round playing brag and solo without a care in the whole darn world. And long before I'd got to doing my solo they'd have packed it in and gone off to their billets.

Inevitably my thoughts shifted to my own billet, which was one of the warmest and the cosiest of all. We'd been lucky, me and Peter

Mitchell, having instead of an iron bed in a hut with a double row of beds, which was what most of the course had to accept, a small room at the end of the hut with just two iron beds in it and a stove of its own. I thought of what Peter was probably doing now: banking the stove up high and leaving its door open so that, nice and snug under the blankets, he could watch the firelight flickering on the walls while he listened to Hoagy Carmichael's 'Stardust' played endlessly on his portable. And then when sleep started taking over, Pete, who'd been imaginative and fixed up a complicated arrangement of strings, would pull on one of them and it would shut the fire door. But by the time I got back the fire would be out and Pete would be asleep, which would be irritating because what I'd want to do was give him two fingers and tell him I was a jump ahead – I'd done my first night solo.

The duty officer called out another name and as another pupil got to his feet I fell to wondering gloomily just how many he had sent to their deaths. It was all too inevitable, all too regular, people killing themselves night-flying. But what else could you expect? An airfield strung between an icy sea on one side and mountains on the other. With sand dunes you had to clear one end in landing and the bloody great Montrose Basin to catch you if you messed it up on take-off. And a bastard of an aircraft like the Master. It was criminal, that's what it was, bloody criminal. They ought to reserve night-flying for moonlit nights. No one pranged on them. And no one . . .

'Kelly!'

I couldn't believe my ears.

'Kelly!' The duty officer's voice was testy.

'Yes, Sir?' I asked.

'Well, get to your feet, man. We haven't got all night.'

I couldn't credit it. What about . . . ? I couldn't remember the name of the pupil who'd been called before me and who was making his way back to the place he'd quitted moments earlier. And what about all the rest of these fellows around me who were in the course ahead of mine. Why pick on me ahead of *them*?

I dared to put it into words.

'I know what course you're on, Kelly,' the duty officer said testily. 'I've got it written down here. Don't keep Flight Lieutenant Mackenzie waiting. Jump to it.'

I struggled to my feet, my body stiff, a crick somewhere in my neck. And I remember even after all these years that as I searched in the gloom for my helmet and the rest of it, my eyes were misted with anger and frustration. It wasn't fair. It just wasn't bloody fair! Why pick on me? Why not at least give me a fair crack of the whip? Quite often when the weather closed in they had to pack it in early and then with any luck the next call didn't come until the moon had started rising. As likely as not that's what would happen tonight – after I'd killed myself!

After that comes the blank. Whether I did my five circuits and bumps with Mackenzie and then immediately did my first night solo or whether there was a period of time between the dual and solo I can't say for sure, but I suspect it was the latter for it was certainly in a different aircraft. There they are in my Log Book: 7620 with Mackenzie and 8002 solo. And I distinctly remember walking out from the hut into the night with the customary 'Good luck', from one or two ringing in my ears.

'Good luck.' The words stayed with me in the dark outside. From the north the wind moaned through the sand dunes, knifing my cheeks, and after the comparative brightness of the dispersal hut the darkness of the night was absolute. Ungainly with the parachute bouncing against my rump, I stumbled out across the grass to the waiting Master guided by the blue pencil light of a torch held by an invisible member of the ground staff. Willing hands helped me up and in. I felt the warmth of a close human body. I would have spoken but I could think of nothing to say. 'Good luck', again. Did they always say that, I wondered?

Pulled tight, the straps over thighs and shoulders were comforting. I slid the cockpit cover shut only to see, to my horror, directly above, about to land on top of me, another aircraft, its green and red navigation lights mere inches above my head! Panic-stricken, I slammed the Perspex cockpit cover open again although it was far too late to get out in time . . . and the aircraft vanished. Sick with relief, I laughed at my own idiocy – for the lights had been my own wingtip lights reflected in the canopy!

Having taxied to the end of the airfield I waited for the green of an Aldis lamp to signal approval for take-off. Ahead of me was a faint line of lights, meanly lit and meanly spaced. These were the well-named glim lamps, low-powered and covered with small hoods so as to be visible only when approaching them from very low altitudes. Apart from them and the cheerful colours of the cockpit lamps there was only blackness. Around me lay the mystery of the airfield. To my left the invisible sea surging steadily against the sandy – or was it shingle? – beach, to my right the wartime station without so much as a glow to advertise its presence to the enemy, and beyond it a narrowish stretch of more or less level land before the Grampians, rising steeply to several thousand feet, began. Behind me were the sand dunes as much as 150 feet high into which only a day or two before for some unaccountable reason Garland had crashed while making his first and only solo night approach; ahead, at the end of the airfield, lay the Montrose Basin, approaching two miles square, that curious stretch of water connected to the ocean by its slender channel into which too many aircraft had crashed through pilot error. Above was the limitless night.

But I was more secure now. Dual and solo I had flown more than eighty hours in Masters, and a hundred and twenty in aircraft altogether, and the familiar feeling of the controls while taxying out had reassured me. Even so I still contemplated with envy the hundreds of men and women who in invisible control towers, messes and billets, were going about their business without fear of what the next ten or twelve minutes might bring. At the same time it was not without a little pride that I reflected that for those ten or twelve minutes what I was doing was what the airfield was all about. That in effect, a thousand and more men and women were at that moment only there at all because of me!

The signal stabbed the darkness underlining the point: mine was the airfield, mine the station's operation. I made the final essential checks: that the mixture control was set to normal rich, the airscrew in fine pitch, the undercarriage and flap levers fully neutral, the various temperatures as they should be, the radiator shutter open, the trim tabs correct.

I opened the throttle, gently pushing it forward to its fullest extent, very conscious of the roundness of its ball against my palm, and I eased the control column forward sufficiently for the tail to be a little below flying position. As the aircraft gathered speed, bumping across the uneven ground, I adjusted the slight tendency to swing away from the meagre line of glim lamps by a touch of rudder. And then, it seemed simultaneously, the bumping ceased and the glim lamps vanished. I was airborne. At once I retracted the undercarriage and from practice born of experience let my hand slip off the throttle onto the large elevator trimming wheel to counteract the feeling of tail-heaviness. I noted with satisfaction the lights of the undercarriage position indicator change from green to red; the wheels were safely locked away. Returning my hand to the throttle lever I shifted my gaze to the vital central instrument panel, which told me the essential things: my airspeed, altitude, rate of climb, my turn and bank, my directional heading and, this most important of all, the artificial horizon, which showed the relationship of the Master to the invisible real horizon. The world outside for the moment did not exist but in this first stage at least, what I had to do was simple: keep the aircraft climbing steadily and levelly until I reached 1,000 feet.

Eyes glued to these instruments, correcting the least flaw in what they advised me with, imaginably, the care and precision of a surgeon conducting the most delicate of operations, my confidence mounted steadily. What I was doing, I reassured myself, was exactly what I had done successfully in Link Trainer exercises. A dozen times cocooned in that strange toy I had taken off and landed an aircraft safely; even better, by picking up different signals I had, theoretically lost in cloud, homed in on radio beacons and put down successfully in thick fog on new and nameless airfields. And a Link Trainer, I reminded himself, was a far more sensitive creature than a Miles Master.

At 1,000 feet I executed a rate-one ninety degree turn crosswind. The Montrose Basin, I reflected, would be directly beneath me now, Dacre and Barkmans's graveyards, (again the names are fictitious) and the graveyard of others in many earlier courses. But the thought failed to bring the expected shaft of fear and for the first time I permitted myself a glance away from my instruments with the vague idea of perhaps seeing the glimmer of water below. But there was nothing to see, nothing but the red and green wingtip lights and blue and yellow flames from the exhausts flickering like marsh gas along the fuselage.

Judging the correct time to make my second turn I brought the Master back along the reciprocal course to take-off onto the downwind leg. I would, I mused, be fairly well out now over the sea, the winter-cold grey North Sea – and I imagined the breakers dying on the beach and I thought about the Scottish girl I had picked up in the dance hall and how we had lain together there, for all that it was very cold, kissing and cuddling but nothing more because in those days most of us were innocents until we married. It was only a flash of a thought, for now it was time to lower the undercarriage. I throttled back a little, and then rather more, my eyes glued to the airspeed indicator and then, when my speed had dropped to less than 150 miles an hour, I reached for the undercarriage lever downside to my left and firmly lowered it. With a sense of infinite satisfaction I felt the crunch of the wheels locking down and saw the red lights vanish from the panel and green lights take their place.

There were only two more turns to make. The turn crosswind when I must reduce speed further to less than 130 miles an hour before lowering the dreaded flaps and then the turn into wind for landing. I made the first, and lowering the flaps compensated for the excess load on the control column as the nose began dropping down by an adjustment of the trimming tabs. I must remember, I told myself, not to allow

17

my speed to drop below eighty miles an hour and especially in that final turn I must keep the nose up with top rudder. I said these things aloud. It was all bookwork stuff. I was a youngster cocooned in a tiny cockpit, trained to accept that so long as I stuck strictly to what the manual and the instructors had told me, there would be no problems.

I made the final turn. A degree of nervousness – for the past few minutes entirely lost in the effort of total concentration – returned. If my timing had been correct I would be heading for the centre of the airfield; if incorrect too much perhaps to one side or the other. But it was broad; there was margin for a reasonable error. Making an engine-assisted approach I started losing height, my eyes darting up from the main instrument panel through the cockpit hood for the first sight of the glide path indicator, then down again to check aircraft attitude and speed. I was talking continually, encouragingly to myself, 'Don't think,' I said, 'you're going to see those glim lamps until you get well down because you won't. Just keep it steady, Kelly, keep it steady.' I was tense but confident, certain I'd made a good job of things. Any moment now . . . yes, there it was! The glide path indicator! Amber! Too high! Should I throttle back or increase the line of attack? I glanced quickly at the airspeed indicator. Not over-much margin there! I pushed the nose down slightly and after moments which seemed to pass with excruciating slowness the amber light abruptly vanished, to be replaced by green. It was a question of good judgement now. I mustn't get too fast, mustn't dive too steeply. Yes, the thing to do now that I'd got the green was ease back on the stick to hold it there. Ease back a trifle, not too much to cause the speed to fall too low but the moment the amber came back, if it did, again ease forward.

'Ah!' I am sure I must have let out a cry of exultation as the line of glim lamps magically materialised, proving my circuit had been accurate, and with an overpowering sense of glee reached for and pulled on the landing lamps lever, but even as the two brilliant beams streamed out, raking the night, proving the solid human world existed, a contrary light flashed at me from the invisible control tower. Red for danger! But it said more, far more than that! It said *Go round again!* I stared at it, horror-stricken. 'Why?' I shouted. 'Why? Why? Why?' The light kept winking, winking red. *Do as you're told. Go round again!* It did not occur to me to disobey. There had to be a reason. Another aircraft in the circuit, maybe? Some obstacle on the ground? I refused to believe the error could be mine.

Chagrined and uneasy, I opened up the throttle and pulled the control column back and at once my rising wingtips hid the flashing Aldis lamp, and the brilliant rays of my landing lights streamed upwards, losing themselves in the inky void above. The Master, until then delightfully smooth and responsive, became a lumbering tank, fighting the braking effect of lowered flaps and wheels. Seizing the undercarriage lever, I rammed it upwards. The reassuring green lights vanished as I pressed against the control column to equate the change of trim. I felt the wheels lock up, saw the red lights flash on and felt the drip of sweat. Now came the danger time. I had to raise the flaps – but if you raised them too quickly the nose would rear and flick you into an incipient spin, corkscrewing you down into the Montrose Basin. As, it was assumed, had happened to Barkmans and Dacre. And over the months many more. The landing lamps streamed on, forgotten; everything but the thought of flaps was obliterated from my mind. I must raise them slowly, fraction by fraction. As I raised them the nose would tend to rise and I must compensate by forward pressure on the stick, and with the other hand feel for the trimming wheel and wind it forward. Gingerly I reached down for the flap lever, a lever smaller than the undercarriage lever but located very near to it, and raised it slightly. The effect was immediate, the aircraft seeming to weigh back against the control column against which my right hand pushed. I slipped my left hand to the trimming wheel and slightly forward. At once the pressure eased. I moved my hand back to the flap lever and raised it a trifle more, pressed against the control column, adjusted the trim. And so it continued until at last it had been achieved, the flaps were fully raised.

It was only then I realised I was soaked in sweat; my body in its sidcot, uniform and underclothes, my hands within three layers of gloves, my head inside the helmet. But I had done it. Succeeded where Dacre and Barkmans had failed. Where others had failed. Weak with relief, I relaxed, and it was only then I saw the beams from my landing lamps raking the night, and swore and hastily switched them off. But how far, I wondered, had I flown? In the relief I was still alive this didn't at first strike me as important but as an interesting question. Had I cleared the Basin? Yes, presumably – it was less than two miles wide. And after the Basin, what? 'There wasn't a problem, was there? There weren't any hills? No, the Grampians were to the right. I turned my head to look through the Perspex canopy for them and to my horror saw two eyes glaring back at me. The immediate effect was as chilling as to a woman who hearing a noise draws back night-curtains to see a face staring in. It took moments for me to realise that the ebony night, made blacker by the glow within the cockpit, turned the cockpit hood into a mirror. That it was useless looking out, that the night was utterly impenetrable. Then the mountains, for all I knew, could be ahead of me! The throttle was still wide open, I'd forgotten all about it, forgotten the engine noise, forgotten everything except the flaps! Forgotten to check my heading!

Immediately an utter certainty that I was heading directly for the Grampians seized me, and at once I hauled the Master round to port and held it there, putting distance between me and the imagined mountains. But then I thought, if I go too far out to sea, I shall lose the land. And I did not know what to do. I began peering, wildly, looking in all directions. And saw nothing. Only blackness. And my own frightened, staring eyes. With sudden surprise I realised the seriousness of my predicament. Without radio contact – for even at night the Masters at No. 8 RAF Flying School, Montrose, were not equipped with radio – I was lost in a pitch-black night, all sense of direction gone, with somewhere the sea, somewhere the mountains and God alone knew where, the airfield!

And now I knew something which was even worse than fear: a sense of devastating loneliness. And blindness – as if sight was limited by the confines of my cockpit.

Panic is a pilot's greatest danger. His security, his hope of returning to the land of living men and women, is utterly dependent on his ability to integrate precise and delicate movements with his hands and feet with the instructions issued by a cool, clear, thinking mind. But panic can utterly destroy the relationship of mind and body, so that the one can be concerned with horrible imaginings while the other thrashes wildly, spurred by instincts which do not necessarily have validity. Moreover, normally the mind has many aids such as sight and recognition which are wanting in total darkness. Night, of course, is never entirely black. Even if there is no moon and a layer of cloud shuts out the stars, the eyes, albeit gradually, adjust so that it may be possible by the application of grim determination and utter concentration eventually just to pick out a faint horizon and use that as a guide. But to achieve this from an aircraft it is essential to destroy such light as you have about you, and specifically your cockpit lights. This, with my lack of experience and in the terrible stress of the moment, I did not think of doing. On the contrary the greens and reds and whites and ambers of the various instruments and navigation lights were a source of comfort, the only proof that I had sight and that a tangible world outside the Master did exist; to plunge myself voluntarily into inky blackness, to, as it were, draw the horrid night into the cockpit itself, even had I thought of doing so, would have been an unimaginable proposition. And so looking this way and that – up, down, sideways – rewarded only by my own desperate face staring back at me, I began to lose control, paying less and less attention to my instruments, to what my hands and feet were doing, driven by the absurd conviction that only my eyes could save me.

It was the sound which rescued me. At first I heard it as no more than a gentle hiss, a weird distraction from the important things on hand. And then it was something more: a feeling of *resistance*. Momentarily abandoning my hopeless peering into vacuum and glancing at the instrument panel, I noticed that my speed had crept higher than it should, while the altimeter told me I was losing height. I found this intensely irritating. I needed all my faculties to spot some pinprick somewhere which would tell me at least if I was over land or sea. I hauled back roughly on the control column to raise the Master's nose and recommenced with steadily mounting desperation my search through the cockpit's Perspex. But the sound persisted; indeed increased.

Glaring angrily at the instruments, I saw to my amazement that my speed was even faster and that not only was I continuing to lose height but the rate of loss of it was increasing. Puzzled enough to have even my growing panic checked, I pulled the control column even further back. But the response was diametrically opposed to what it should have been. My speed grew faster still, my altimeter showed a continuing loss of height. Baffled, I stared at the control column, now pulled back well beyond the vertical. By all the laws which governed flight I should have been climbing steeply, there might even be risk of stalling! I pulled back further still – yet still the speed increased, still the altimeter needle continued its anti-clockwise course. Amazed, I saw that the airspeed counter had travelled fully round the dial and was commencing its second turn, was indicating a speed significantly faster than that of normal level flight. My eyes flicked down to the altimeter: 650 feet and falling, not just steadily but fast. I stared, bewildered while my ears were filled with the sound of rushing night.

And then it came to me. There had been a vast miscalculation. There were circumstances in which the standard rules which governed flight ceased to apply. It explained so much. Others had met these circumstances – planes had vanished without trace and logical explanations had been sought to account for their disappearance. And this was all it was. How simple. How very simple. Allenby of twenty-five course. Even Garland, possibly. Suddenly they had found themselves as I was now – a Phaethon no longer in control. I watched the dials and a curious dispassion came over me. The speed was faster still, the height below 500 feet with the altimeter needle having passed through the lowest point on the dial now moving evenly upwards, moving up to zero feet. I realised that very soon I would be dead. There would be another muffled thump and another ball of yellow flame and if it so happened that my crash was near the airfield, those still due to fly would quit dispersal and put up with the cold to stare for a few moments at my funeral pyre – as I had stared at Garland's. And what was interesting was that, of a sudden, fear was quite gone. The situation was unchangeable; I had done what I'd been taught to do and done it, I was sure, correctly. If the Gods chose to play a little game sometimes and alter the rules of flight so that aircraft did the exact reverse of what they should be doing, ordinary mortals had no choice but to accept the consequences of their little joke.

Inexplicably the cheerful colours of the cockpit lights put me in mind of the one and only cocktail party I had attended. I couldn't quite see the connection yet the sense of it was very real. I leaned back against the seat, enjoying the recollection. It was not that I could actually bring to mind visions of other people, see the faces of men or girls I'd briefly met, it was just that the noise I could hear and the gay friendly lights about me were strangely analogous to the hum of conversation, and the colours to the colours of drinks in glasses, and their warmth to the feeling of companionship. Yet at the same time this was curious because the sound was anything but the same, for this sound was the scream of slipstream along the fuselage – a sound which, it seemed to me, was of a moving thing which would never stop but would continue into the endlessness of time when all there would be left of me would be bloody bits of bone mingled with cogs and wires and twisted metal.

And I experienced a calm I could not remember experiencing before. In a few moments I would be dead – and it hardly seemed worth the effort to wonder what dying would be like.

I allowed my eyes to drift across the instruments – and all at once saw that the artificial horizon had toppled, the turn-and-bank was at a crazy angle and the gyro-compass spinning so fast its figures were indecipherable. For perhaps fifty of my precious remaining feet I stared open-mouthed, shaken from my torpor, seeing my machine as it really was, not as some uncontrollable meteor hurled by the Gods but as a Master aircraft tight-turning in a dipping circle, its navigation lights cutting a falling path like the coil of a spring. What I had done was utterly simple. Neglecting my instruments I had, unknowingly, put on bank; through my failing to keep the nose up with top rudder it had dropped and a gentle turn had begun. By pulling back on the control column, far from correcting this I had merely tightened the turn and thus increased the speed and loss of height still further. In daylight, even at night with a good horizon, correction would have been instinctive, automatic, but with nothing against which to relate myself, and with my mind occupied with anything but what it should have been, my presumed corrections had merely snowballed the original error. The elevators were no longer acting to raise the nose but had become rudders tightening the turn and the more the turn was tightened the less lift the mainplanes provided. Had I but known it, at that moment it was a toss-up whether I would have crashed while still in my diving turn or as the result of flicking into an incipient spin.

My reaction was instinctive and immediate. With both hands clamped hard on the control column I hauled it sideways, taking off the bank. My mind was very clear, for there hadn't been time for returning fear to cloud it, and thoughts of death were banished. I must, I knew, be very careful. The altimeter showed a mere 250 feet; only exquisite judgement could extract me from my predicament. Fighting the temptation to do otherwise, I pushed forward on the stick. Hauled back as it had been the turning would have been translated into a sudden climb with the risk of stall; yet at the same time the Master was in a falling pattern which the correction of the controls would not immediately amend. There was a sinking factor which it took time to overcome. Taking my left hand off the control column I shoved the throttle forward to its maximum position, increasing boost, and, feeling the welcome surge of power, brought back the stick the merest trifle. Now there was little to do but wait – and hope. I dared not look at my altimeter; I did not look at it. Instead I concentrated on my turn-and-bank. The one thing I could do to assist survival was keep the Master level; the rest lay with the Gods. And I knew there were only moments left in which my fate would be decided. Either my corrections had been made in time for the downward drift to be halted or I would belly into the land or sea below.

Somewhere down below, his hands rammed into his greatcoat pockets, the Duty Officer, whose name I do not know, would have been watching. Although to me the time since take-off was half a lifetime, in fact it would still have been only a matter of minutes, and the time between my going round again and now still less. Consequently, by turning to port as sharply as I had and keeping the turn going long enough to feel sure the mountains must be behind my back, I had (as I was later to be informed) actually brought the Master back to a point where, when I began my tight diving turn, I was over the very sand dunes where Garland had killed himself two days before.

And realising from the sound of it that something serious was amiss, the Duty Officer would have hastily squeaked back his chair and hurried out, followed by the majority of the pupils yet to fly, to be greeted by the sight, crisply illuminated by its red and green wingtip lights, of an aircraft performing the most amazing gyrations. Experienced pilot though he was, as he was later to remark, he had never seen the like of it before nor ever hoped to see the like of it again. Anything but a case-hardened man (he loathed his drafting to Montrose as an instructor) he had been only too conscious when Garland had killed himself that it was he who had sent him out to his death, and after it had happened had, so I was told, taken it on himself to suggest to the Station Commanding Officer that flying should be suspended for that night. Unable to prevail, he now faced the awful prospect of a repeat calamity about which he could do absolutely nothing.

It is not difficult to imagine him. The snarl of the Master's Kestrel engine must have drowned that of the surging sea, and the biting wind would be chilling him unheeded. He would be oblivious to the knot of youngsters standing aghast a yard or two behind him, his head moving to follow its terrifying arcs, as he stared with fascinated horror at the ghastly, yet comical performance being executed before his very eyes. Not for an instant would it have occurred to him that the idiot flying that Master had abandoned all hope of surviving. But, as I was later told, it did occur to him, hopefully, that perhaps the Master was unoccupied, that the fool of its pilot had for some reason baled out. And the more he considered this possibility, the more he came to believe in it, so that he was torn between waiting for the crash and hurrying back into the dispersal hut to alert the station. And then, as if magically, the Master righted itself, and taking a course roughly reciprocal to its take-off run, its engine snarling even louder, skimmed over the top of the sand dunes and, beginning a gentle climb, headed northwards.

I wonder what his thoughts were as he stared after it. It would have been hardly less credible had some phantom aircraft performed what he had seen performed. I imagine him shaking his head, his eyes still following the fading lights, only then becoming aware of the gabble of voices from behind him, and turning swiftly, shouting: 'Get inside! All of you!' And, seeing the yellow light spilling out from the opened door of the dispersal hut: 'And shut that door after you! Don't you know there's a bloody war on!'

They would have gone in unwillingly, and when someone shut the door and he found himself abruptly plunged into blackness he might have regretted having given the order. Still watching the receding navigation lights and listening to the receding engine hum, he would have searched for cigarettes, and having with some difficulty lit one, stayed out on the desolate, windswept, snow-scattered airfield.

Just as when I'd found myself in the situation described in the previous chapter, my gut reaction to eluding death by a hair's-breadth was to put as much space between myself and the ground as possible. My eyes, glued to the instrument panel, darted from turn-and-bank to altimeter to rate-of-climb to airspeed indicator like those of a cornered animal seeking some avenue of escape, and in a plethora of impatience I prayed for the artificial horizon I had toppled in my wild manoeuvrings to right itself, as eventually it would.

Events crowding one on top of another and the sheer concentration I was applying to the immediate things on hand blotted out the sense of relief I might otherwise have felt at finding myself still alive. I did not for the moment even consciously think in terms of being in an aircraft at all, of there being a night outside, of the existence of other humans – the world had shrunk to the story being told by two square feet of metal plate pierced by six circular dials and the relationship of the story they were telling to my hands on throttle and control column and my feet on rudder bar. My body was ramrod-tense, as were my bent arms and legs; not out of apprehension but because having once found how to hold the pointers in the required positions I locked my limbs to keep them exactly there. In effect both mentally and physically I made of myself a robot.

With a kind of grim satisfaction I saw the altimeter crawling upwards. For some reason the magic height to be reached was 1,000 feet and it was only when this had been attained that peripheral thoughts began to intrude. The first of these was the realisation that I hadn't the least idea of where in the world – or more as it seemed to me, where in the universe – I was; and the second, which swiftly ousted the first, where the Grampians were. Well, I advised myself, the thing to do is to continue for the time being exactly as I am until, if I haven't hit them first, I've cleared them. I couldn't remember exactly how high they rose except that I thought it wasn't above 3,000 feet. Nevertheless, for good measure, I decided to climb to four.

Thinking revived apprehension but the lessons learnt from the result of allowing fear to rule now enforced a better discipline. Stiff as an automaton, head thrust forward almost to the windscreen as if its being two or three inches nearer would give me that little extra time for taking evasive action, oblivious to the engine's note or drop in cockpit temperature as I climbed, I stared at my own eyes reflected in the Perspex canopy and braced my body for the half-expected collision. When it failed to come and the altimeter tidily confirmed the objective had been achieved, for the first time I relaxed and, levelling out, took stock of the situation.

It was, as I saw it, a pretty hopeless one. I had been flying, I imagined, for about half an hour (in fact it would have been far less) and I might be anything up to a hundred miles distant from Montrose, perhaps even more. Below me would almost certainly be either snow-capped mountain tops or a cold grey sea and there was no possible way of discovering which it was of these two equally unpleasant alternatives. Nor was there any way I could communicate with the world below or for the world below to communicate with me. In plain I was on my own the best part of a mile up in the sky, hopelessly lost with a limited time to find the answer before I ran out of fuel.

I could of course bale out – but the prospect of ending my life in the slow, solitary death of exposure on a mountain top or by drowning in an icy sea were both equally appalling. In any case I had begun to feel a bond between myself and the machine which, while everything else was beyond my power to control, was responsive to my commands, and the thought of abandoning the comfort and reassurance of the comparatively warm and well-lit cockpit and projecting myself alone into the inhospitable, empty darkness was anything but appealing.

I thought of God. I remembered a boyhood discussion with another boy named Smith, who had the nickname 'Aggie' (because his initials were A.G.), who had been quite devout. In a discussion at a school camp we'd both attended, Aggie Smith had rejected my atheism out of hand and assured me with sweeping confidence that the time would come when I would suddenly find myself facing a crisis and then I would discover that after all, I did believe, and I would call on God for help and it would be given. Well, I supposed, there was no harm in trying and I did in fact say out aloud something like: 'Well, God, if ever I need some help it's now. Just tell me what to do.' But I was aware there was no conviction in it and wasn't surprised when no voice instructed me nor angels' wings appeared out of the night to flutter me and aircraft safely down.

My state of mind was by now quite different from anything in my previous experience. Accepting that I was almost certainly going to die but not for a good half hour and possibly longer, fear, if not entirely conquered, had been subdued by a fatalistic composure in which I was able to study calmly the possibilities still open to me and recall such advice as had been given during training.

'What are you supposed to do when lost?' I seemed to hear a voice asking me.

'You do a square search.'

'And what, Kelly, is a square search exactly?'

'Well, you pick a direction in which to fly and keep on it for a fixed length of time, two minutes say, and then you turn through ninety degrees, fly for another two minutes, turn again and so on until you've done a box and are more or less back where you started from. Then you start making another box next to that one and so on until you find something that's going to solve your problem.'

Yes, that was all very well – in daylight. But what would I be searching for *now*? A glimmer of light? A glimmer of light could equally be escaping from the carelessly pulled blackout curtain of a lowland cottage or mountainside hut; or from some ship far out at sea!

No, I told myself, the only hope left to me is to find Montrose airfield. And if I can't do that, then, horrible though the thought of it is, I'm going to have to bale out and hope to hell this Master doesn't crash-land on a hospital or something. So I've got what? I glanced at the fuel contents indicators, one for each wing tank. Well, at least half an hour, I suppose. Enough for about three square searches. All right, I decided, that's what I'd do. Three square searches, two minutes each leg and then if I haven't spotted someone flashing an Aldis lamp at me or something, out I go into, and I said it aloud, 'into that bloody Stygian abyss!'

I was aided now by the artificial horizon, which had recovered so that I had the mock aircraft to indicate the relationship of my Master to the invisible real horizon. But I made two mistakes; one of which I was to realise quite soon, the other not at all. The sensible thing would have been first to fly on a reciprocal course to that which I had taken on my long slow climb, so as to locate myself approximately where I'd started out before beginning the first of my square searches. The problem was that, having little belief I was likely to achieve anything in aimlessly tooling round the sky using up what little petrol I'd still got, but, grimly determined at least to do what my elders and betters had instructed, I had determinedly put out of my mind everything but the job on hand. I looked at the heading shown by the gyro-compass, glanced at the time-of-flight clock, and banking the Master into a meticulously rate-one turn, held it thus for precisely ninety degrees before levelling out and setting off on the first of my four two-minute legs. It was only when halfway down the second of these I realised my error, by which time compensating would have been far too complex a problem. If needs be, I thought, the first search has to be wasted; when it's finished I'll do that reciprocal course for what? – well, it was a guess, ten minutes – and then I'll start again.

The second mistake was caused by doing something which I ought to have done before and then going over the top on it. Of a sudden, thinking about glimmers of light or Aldis lamps flashing at me from below, I realised that I'd be more likely to see them if I dimmed my cockpit lights to the minimum. And, having done this and been rewarded by the merciful disappearance of my own reflection in the hood, I went over the top and decided to make an even better job of it by switching off my navigation lights.

Now, for the first time since I had taken off, I had time to meditate. The comparative warmth of the cockpit, the steady engine hum, the flickering exhaust flames, the dim glow of the navigation instruments, the reality of control column to hand and rudder bar to feet, the growing conviction that while it was sensible to do what I was doing there was really little purpose in it, the very feeling of being cut off from earthly influences, combined to create a frame of mind in which were elements of resignation, self-criticism and regret. I was sure I was going to die and was saddened more than afraid. There were so many things I had yet to do, so many ambitions unfulfilled. And the greatest of these, perhaps, was to break my duck with a girl – to make love properly. It seems strange now when I look back on it that under such circumstances such a thought should be uppermost in my mind – but this was in the early forties when we were so very innocent, when not one man in twenty learning to fly (if as many) had actually had sex with a girl and the thought of doing so baulked strongly in one's mind as a great ambition one day to be fulfilled. So I thought of girls I had known and soon of the girl I had necked with on Montrose beach, the last girl I had had sexual contact with or ever would again. And I thought of a girl I knew at home I'd convinced myself I was in love with. There was no connection in my mind between these two girls. My nature was such as to divide women into two categories – those one could have sex with (if one had the courage to suggest it and the good fortune to be accepted) and those who were not so much untouchable as not to be touched. From the second I drew the romantic concepts on which I based my aspirations, from the first I drew my modest sexual fantasies – but as yet I hadn't met a girl who would allow me to indulge them all the way. I'd talked this over with Pete and he'd been encouraging. 'Don't worry, Terry,' he'd said. 'You just wait till you've got your wings – they'll be throwing themselves at you. I bet the very first leave when you've got your wings up you'll break your duck.'

It had been a delightful prospect but now I wouldn't be getting my wings after all and that was the next most important ambition which would never be fulfilled. From inspection I'd seen that a pilot's brevet opened doors which had been closed, admitted one to a brotherhood envied by all who could not be part of it, gave the wearer self-assurance and so far as girls were concerned, worked magic. I suppose we all have something of a Walter Mitty in us and I had often imagined myself fully-fledged, smart in uniform, sergeant's or officer's, brevet on breast, top button undone to show I was a fighter pilot (if that was what they had chosen me to be), ordering dinner and wine in romantic restaurants while across candlelit tables pretty girls in off-the-shoulder evening dresses gazed at me adoringly. Well, it was not to be; not that, nor the daredevil exploits in Spitfire or Hurricane, or the long tense flights over enemy territory in Halifax or Lancaster, nor the binges with my kind in the Regent Palace Hotel in Piccadilly, which was apparently where aircrew met on leave, nor any of the other vague imaginings which had filled my daydreams. It was not to be, none of it, because I'd made a mess of things. I'd been given my chance and botched it. Had been so focussed on managing the simple matter of raising a Master's flaps as to have completely overlooked the possibility of disorientating myself. And having got lost had all but crashed by ignoring a bevy of instruments there to tell me exactly what I was doing. The simple fact of the matter, I told myself, was that I was, in this, as I had shown myself to be in other ways, inept. I'd had no business putting myself forward as aircrew and in the extremely unlikely event I, by some miracle, survived I would have myself reclassified.

A train of thoughts if not exactly as these, certainly close to them, occupied my mind through my first square search and along the reciprocal leg of my climb away from Montrose, and by an odd co-incidence I really *had* just reached the decision to give up the idea of being a pilot if the miracle occurred, when I saw the flare. It was faint and far away, a greenish glow which grew, hesitated, fell away in a curious trajectory and died. I did not at once connect it with myself, in fact saw it rather as in normal times I might have seen a shooting star; it was only when, after an interval of perhaps two minutes I saw another, this time nearer and seeming to climb higher up towards me, that I realised what it was. That someone was firing cartridges from a Very pistol.

The events of this traumatic first night solo had combined to give a disproportionate relevance to everything with which I was concerned as, I suppose, had been evidenced by the almost puritanical precision of my flying from the moment when I recovered self-control, and as soon as I saw the flare for what it was, a homing beacon, the thought of Aggie Smith flashed through my mind. And in much the same way as a penitent reads approval in subsequent happenings which benefit

29

him, so I saw a direct connection between the flare and my decision to have myself reclassified as groundstaff. It was as if the Gods, objecting to an incompetent careering round their firmament and determined to be rid of him, had unbent on discovering he was going to quit it voluntarily.

It all made sense to me at the time and dissipated the last shreds of fear. It did not occur to me at all that the tremendous stresses I had borne were still affecting me, nor that I was actually handling an aircraft now with greater expertise than I had ever before; and even had I done so I imagine I would have quite failed to see there was an arrant contradiction between this and my decision to be done with flying. And what still lay ahead of me before I finally put the Master safely down on Montrose airfield did nothing to persuade me to change my mind.

Inexperienced airline passengers are confused, and often quite alarmed, when, on a flight made at night, their pilot, following unknown ground instructions, instead of making a direct approach circles the airfield at a lowish level. Instead of their first sight of the flare path being a line of brilliant lights beside which they will very shortly touch down, they may suddenly see this necklace above the level of their heads, seeming to indicate they are flying, if not upside-down, at least in the most peculiar of attitudes. And as they watch, their sense of disorientation increases as this line of lights, appearing to be a movable axis, continually changes its direction, sometimes apparently diving underneath the aircraft, at others angled upwards to the heavens. The explanation is, of course, quite simple: however steep the bank of their aircraft, securely strapped in their seats and with the world outside their tiny windows black, everything they see around them inside the aircraft appears to be on a level and horizontal plane while anything they may chance to see outside which is in fact horizontal appears to be at an angle of some sort. But then by some magic the pilot sorts things out, persuades the flare path to behave itself and lie down decently where it ought to, makes his approach and lands. Apprehension is set aside and, in the business of extracting hand baggage and inching uncomfortably towards the exit doors, soon forgotten. And after a few more night landings the passenger either doesn't bother about it or gets the hang of things and accepts, or even loses all interest in what is no longer a phenomenon.

On this, my second attempt to put the Master down, I was in a similar, but somewhat worse, situation in that instead of being able to comfort myself with the reflection that however odd things seemed to be, here were a few hundred fellow passengers who were clearly quite at ease and instead of there being, somewhere up front, a trained crew (who must obviously know what they are doing or they'd have killed themselves long ago), mine was the problem and there was no one to help me sort it out. I had been trained to fly on instruments and to expect my first sight of the flare path to be at a time when I was more or less flying parallel to it and descending at an angle onto which I'd been directed by the glide path indicator. But now, as I changed my course and dropped the aircraft's nose to head directly towards the latest signal, I suddenly saw, as if by magic, a row of pearls appear in the sky above me. I hadn't known that Montrose was equipped with a perfectly normal peacetime flare path; I don't suppose any of us knew it. Now in the desperate circumstances that some fool of a pupil was blundering around up above, obviously lost and at his wits end to know what to do, the station Commanding Officer had had no alternative but to 'risk the presence of a stooging Dornier or Heinkel and turn the blasted things full on!'

Astonished by this sudden manifestation, I stared at it for some moments before recognising it for what it had to be and at once, instinctively (as well might have the tyro airline passenger had he been in my flying boots) put on bank and climb to compensate. But now in my state of numbed calm, very much on the alert so far as at least my instruments were concerned, I soon realised my error and, correcting it, restored the chain of lights more or less to their original position.

This, however, merely delayed rather than removed the problem. With 4,000 feet to lose before getting down to the proper circuit height the question of making a direct approach and landing did not arise, and long before I was sufficiently low I had passed over the flare path and it had vanished below the belly of the Master, and when I banked to bring it into view again it was to discover it now running in a totally different and quite perplexing direction. And so for quite some time it continued. Whenever I changed my aircraft's attitude the row of lights gyrated crazily. Now they ran from some point in the sky to disappear beneath me as if into some hole in the ground; now, momentarily, they vanished only to reappear on my other side. Sometimes when I forced them straight and parallel, they were too high and seemed to be running level with me, or even above so that I was looking up at them, whilst at others they stretched ahead like an angled hill. I realised perfectly well where the problem lay but found it extraordinarily difficult to divorce myself from looking at it back to front. I could not rid myself of the feeling that I was fixed and the lights were moving. Even while I understood perfectly clearly that all that was required was the application of commonsense, I found myself trying to solve the enigma as if it were one of the exercises in three-dimensional geometry I had found so difficult at school.

However, eventually, almost accidentally perhaps, placing the flare path in a relationship with myself that I could grapple with, I saw how to do so. Of a sudden everything slotted into place and the puzzle was a simple one to solve, indeed not a puzzle any longer. I had passed through the barrier of confusion and in doing so, become a relatively experienced night-flying pilot. Meticulously correct at the very end, I did not immediately attempt to force the Master down but flew at the stipulated 1,000 feet above the flare path, made the necessary turns, across, down and across wind again, lowered undercarriage and flaps at the proper times and picking up the glide path indicator, switched on my landing lights, made a respectable landing and taxied to the dispersal point.

None of this changed the decision I had made to give up flying. I saw in my landing lights, before I remembered to switch them off, the small gaggle awaiting me. I had made an utter fool of myself and I was going to get one hell of a wigging now, and by the morning there wouldn't be a soul on the station who wasn't aware what a Charlie I'd made of things; and my standing amongst my fellow pupils would be rock-bottom. By some miracle I had escaped disaster and it would be both ungrateful and idiotic to imagine I could do so a second time.

Climbing out of the cockpit I paused for a moment to stare up at the inky sky. That line or two of Air Force doggerel crossed my mind: 'Only birds and fools fly, and birds don't fly at night.' How true, I thought – but the difference is that this fool isn't going to fly by daylight either. And wrenching the helmet from my head I walked up to the small group to face the strictures.

There were none.

Flight Lieutenant Mackenzie was the only one to speak.

'Come into the hut for a moment, Kelly,' he ordered. I followed him into the bare, cold, empty dispersal hut. My exploits, it seemed, had caused flying to be cancelled for that night.

'Are you alright?'

'Yes, Sir.'

'Do you want to talk about it?'

'I'd rather not, Sir.'

Mackenzie would have understood. He was sufficiently experienced. The boy's probably shellshocked, he'd have been thinking. There'd be a reaction later. But the worst thing was to bottle up such experiences. The best thing to do was talk them through; not dwell on them in solitude. He set about saying as much.

'I can see that, Kelly,' he said. 'But you know . . .' He paused, searching for the most helpful words.

'I'm sorry to have been such a nuisance, Sir,' I said.

Mackenzie nodded gratefully. 'Well, you have been rather.' He pointed to the ceiling. 'Flying Officer Shipman's still up there looking for you and I don't mind telling you, you nearly gave us all down here heart failure.' He hesitated but I suppose he couldn't resist it. 'When you were carrying out that most impressive steep diving turn, do you know where you were?'

'No, Sir.'

'Over the sand dunes. You must have cleared them by fifty feet at best. Remarkable. You're a very lucky man.' I suppose he felt he had gone off the rails and muffed his opportunity. 'Best thing you can do,' he suggested gruffly, 'is get your chums to bring you a couple of double scotches and then get a good night's sleep. We'll talk about it in the morning.'

Had it been Shipman in the dispersal hut, I would have told him I'd decided to throw in the towel so far as being a pilot was concerned. For a moment I thought about telling Mackenzie now, but what was to me at the time a dizzy rank defeated me.

'Yes, Sir,' I said.

I was run across to the mess in a Commer. It was quiet and the question of having a drink didn't arise and when I went to the hut instead Peter Mitchell wasn't there. I can't remember why. I didn't mind. I sat on the edge of my bed and for a moment or two everything seemed to go purple. But it soon passed. As did my decision to give up flying. Although it had seemed a lifetime doing my first solo it had only taken forty minutes – that's the figure in my Log Book. But forty minutes for a first night solo is a long time. Maybe I broke the Montrose record. I certainly gained a transient notoriety – which is great for a youngster trying to hold his own amongst contemporaries.

I did some more night-flying at Montrose, two batches of it, including eight solo circuits and bumps. And then later I did some night-flying in a Hurricane. Some was on dark nights and some on moonlit nights – and flying solo on a moonlit night is magical and entrancing. With both sets of conditions I never had any trouble – but when a suggestion was put to me I might like to join a night-fighter squadron, I firmly turned it down.

COLLECTING FIR CONES

ITEM Number 14 in the 'Sequence of Instruction' for flying Master aircraft was 'Low Flying (With Instructor Only).' The three words in parentheses were there advisedly for it is probable that, second only to night-flying, the largest number of fatal accidents at Montrose – and no doubt at other training stations – came about through pupils trying their hand at this exercise either solo or accompanied by another pupil.

To my mind flying low in a powerful aircraft (and the Master with its Rolls-Royce Kestrel engine was in this category) can provide the greatest thrill that life can offer. Aerobatics are impressive and exciting but (except when carried out at a low level) do not hold a candle to low flying at or below treetop level. It is impossible to explain why this is so – one has to know the experience personally to be aware of the wonderful sense of speed, power and control which really low flying brings. And there is something else: a feeling of distinction: for the moment one has quitted the rut of normal life and entered a realm which one almost feels one is sharing with the Gods.

And therein at a training station lies the danger, for young men in their prime enjoy appreciation of their prowess by their contemporaries, and how better to earn this than by demonstrating their skill and courage while cocking a snook at rules and regulations.

Item Number 19 in the 'Sequence of Flying' was 'Instrument Flying' – in other words flying by use of instruments rather than by sight; an essential exercise, as may be gathered from my experiences in the two previous chapters. However, sitting in the front of a two-seater aircraft while his pupil, cocooned under a hood, eyes glued to the turn-and-bank and the rest of the instruments, does the flying, is to an instructor a wearisome occupation and the powers who settled the training syllabus had decided that (once the instructor felt his charges sufficiently capable) relief could be given by requiring a second pupil to sit in for him thus, incidentally, releasing him to carry out further dual training.

And so pairs of pupils flew together, with one regarded as captain of the aircraft and the other (dubbed 'Safety Pilot') as passenger.

Whichever was captain would take off the aircraft and fly it to a desig-
nated area and when this had been reached the pupil in the rear would
pull the hood up over him and commence the instrument-flying
exercise.

It has always surprised me that this procedure was adopted, for it is
screamingly obvious that not only would the fellow not under the hood
find this as boring a business as had the instructor whose place he had
taken, but it opened the door wide to temptation. Here, as at no other
time, was the opportunity for Johnny Bold to show William Timid
what a dashing and clever chap he was.

The pupil with whom I did most of this under-the-hood exercise was
named Wilson. I seem to remember he had ginger hair – or perhaps it
is that I associate ginger hair with hotheadedness. I was to fly in the Far
East with an American named Campbell who was nicknamed 'Red'
because of the colour of his hair, and he was unquestionably the most
reckless and foolhardy (as well as the bravest) man I ever met. Anyway,
Wilson certainly had his share of dare-devilry. After a few minutes of
my tooling around under the hood on our first joint flight, he suggested
through the speaking tube (which was the only means by which we
could communicate) that this was a pretty boring operation and why
didn't we go off to the low-flying area and do a 'beat-up' or two.

So that is what we did, with Wilson, who was in the front seat, doing
the flying. It was soon only too apparent that Wilson's notion of what
a 'beat-up' comprised was quite different from mine. I had envisaged
pretending we were fighter pilots attacking some airfield or troops on
the march and doing a few mock-dives and climb-outs. But not a bit
of it. For the next quarter of an hour or so, I was subjected to the most
nerve-wracking moments of my life. Wilson's idea of a beat-up
included flying at almost zero feet and when faced by trees hardly a
wingspan apart, at the last moment hauling the stick sideways to put
the Master in a steep turn and so pass between them. Even worse was
his predilection when over open country to perform tight turns at a
breathtaking and terrifyingly low altitude.

I indicated earlier that the Miles Master possessed nasty habits. One
of the worst of these was, when put under too much pressure in a steep
turn, to flick into an incipient spin.

In the manual for flying a 'Miles Master 1' under the section 'Hints
on Handling' this is covered by what at first reads more like a hint than
a warning but with hindsight more like an excuse:

> It is well known that when an aircraft is in a tight vertical turn pulling
> the control column hard back results in increasing the acceleration and

35

consequently puts up the stalling speed considerably. On aircraft with high wing loadings [as was the Master] this is particularly noticeable. For instance if when flying at 200 m.p.h. the pilot goes into a tight vertical turn and pulls hard back on the control column, the aircraft will very quickly flick or partially roll out of the turn and this may result in a considerable loss of height.

For the 'quickly flick' mentioned above it would be more accurate to have written 'quickly flick into an incipient spin'. In fact just before the Master was so stressed as to flick into this spin a warning juddering of the aircraft occurred which could immediately be eased by taking off a trifle of the bank or which could be increased at one's peril by tightening the turn.

Loss of height (as mentioned in the manual) is of small importance when a pilot has plenty of height to lose – when he has, as was Wilson's wont, perhaps 100 feet maximum, or even less, death is lurking in the wings.

So there we were with full engine power, turning steeply with the wingtip on the inside of the turn seeming to be almost boring a hole in the earth below, and the Master juddering like a car driven in a grossly incorrect gear and death only instants away should Wilson ever so slightly overcook what he was about.

I was frankly terrified. Had I been more mature I would have yelled at Wilson through the speaking tube not to be such a bloody fool, that if he wanted to kill himself that was his business, but please to leave me out of it! But of course at twenty years of age, and at that stage of one's flying career this was something one simply couldn't do; one had to grit one's teeth and hope that the Flight Commander selected someone else for one to do the under-the-hood flying with next time.

It didn't work out like that. It so happened that we were due to have a Navigation Test in a couple of days' time and so, on the very same day, 9 January 1941, in the very same aircraft, Master M7678, we were told to go and do some more instrument flying but this time with the roles reversed. And of course there had to be an unspoken under-standing between Wilson and myself that this time I should be the one to do the 'beat-up'. There was, as I saw it at the time, no escape from it. So after perfunctory under-the-hood flying by Wilson, off we went to the low-flying area and, unenthusiastically – and probably nothing like as dangerously – I did my share of flying between trees much too close together for my liking and executing turns that were also, for my liking, much too near the ground and much too steep, with the Master juddering in its now familiar way. And then, on the very next day, with our Navigation Tests looming, Wilson and I were detailed to do more under-the-hood flying and of course repeated the previous day's fool-hardiness.

On 11 January I had my navigation test and presumably – and understandably – failed to satisfy Flying Officer King, who tested me for I see in my Log Book that on the twelfth I'm under the hood again. This time it was in Master T8437 and it was not with Wilson but with one George Willis. I remember being very pleased about this because I feared that if I flew any more with Wilson (as in fact I had to a few days later) our luck was bound to run out, and Willis was a quiet, sober, sensible fellow.

However, I had discounted the pressure which is insidiously exerted on young men who have to give account of themselves amongst their contemporaries.

On each occasion following our low-flying exercises, honour being satisfied, Wilson and I would have returned to Montrose possessed by the kind of exaltation one knows after a frightening roller-coaster ride has ended and it would have been beyond our self-control not to have boasted a little about it. In any event Willis certainly knew of it, for after we had carried out a respectable stint of under-the-hood flying he felt constrained to suggest, circumspectly, that we repaired to the low flying area, and did a modest 'beat-up' or two.

I doubt if I received this suggestion enthusiastically, but I could hardly negate it and so off we set.

Willis's idea of a 'beat-up' was as chalk to cheese compared with Wilson's. Having brought the Master down to a respectably low alti-tude he proceeded to fly a straight and level course across a series of fields, each divided from the next by a stone wall, and as he approached each wall (although he would unquestionably have cleared it anyway) he lifted the Master up and over it like a well-trained and good-mannered steeplechaser. It was all very pleasant and restful and, much relieved, seated as passenger in the rear I watched the countryside passing by close below us, much as one might from a railway carriage. At some point I noted ahead of us, at quite a consid-erable distance, a wood, and thought to myself: well, to clear those trees Willis is going to have to lift the Master up a bit more than he's doing at the moment. A little later it occurred to me that if he didn't start doing this soon he wasn't going to clear them – and seconds later I *knew* he wasn't going to.

One moment all was blue skies and sunshine, the next moment all was green and then we were back into clear air again. My bubble of relief at having got away with flying through the top of a line of fir trees unscathed was quickly pricked by an anguished cry from Willis:

'What are we going to do!!!?'

I had no idea what was bothering him. 'Fly back to Montrose,' I replied. 'We've done enough under-the-hood for one day.'

'Look at the wings!! Look at the wings!!'

I looked at the wings – and discovered they presented a remarkable and horrifying sight. The Master was mainly of wooden construction and the wings and fuselage plywood, covered with fabric; and some of this fabric, torn by the contact with the branches, was trailing like lavatory paper on a newlywed couple's departing car. And there were holes in the places from which it trailed.

I had no sooner absorbed this alarming phenomenon than I heard another despairing cry:

'I can't hold her up! I can't keep her level.'

Instrument Board of the Miles Master 1. Vital instruments in centre panel reading clockwise: Airspeed Indicator, Artificial Horizon, Rate-of-Climb Indicator, Turn-and-Bank Indicator, Directional Gyroscope, Altimeter.

I saw what he meant. One wing was tilted towards the ground. Through the holes in the mainplanes we were lacking lift on the side where the holes were largest.

'Give me a hand! Give me a hand!'

I grabbed the stick and found it extraordinarily heavy. With noticeable effort I helped Willis pull back on it and shift it to the side of the cockpit. Remarkably the effect of this joint effort was to keep the aircraft flying straight and level.

So there we were, miles away from our airfield, with an aircraft which would not by the normal use of controls turn to the left.

Poor Willis was in a state. As first pilot he was responsible for what had happened. And it was really all my fault, not his.

'What are we going to do?'

'Go back to Montrose.'

'How?'

'We can slew her with the rudder. Try it'

So we did. And, after a fashion it worked – although it made for very awkward flying.

However, as we steered a crablike course back to Montrose other problems presented themselves – the first of these was that the airspeed indicator read zero. This, we were to discover afterwards, was because we'd knocked off the pitot head, which is a small attachment to the leading edge of a wing into which air is driven through an orifice and thus, through the pressure exerted, forces the dial on the instrument round. Not knowing one's airspeed is discomforting, but faced with the knowledge that with so much lift lost our stalling speed had to be higher than normal, the prospect of trying to make a landing (in the dark, as it were, so far as our approach speed was concerned) was disturbing.

Equally disturbing was the behaviour of our radiator temperature gauge. This had begun to climb, slowly but inexorably, upwards. Why it was doing this we could not imagine but doing it, it was, and when it reached boiling point the engine would seize and all we'd have left was our gliding capacity, much limited by the loss of lift. Thus time limitation was added to our problems. And (as the writers of melodrama know only too well, as is evinced by the well-known scene of the lady tied to the railway line as the milk train approaches) there is little which is more nerve-wracking than knowing you have a limited time at your disposal before disaster strikes.

So here are two only moderately experienced twenty-year-olds nervously watching the radiator temperature gauge, both hands clamped on the stick hauled back and rammed hard against one side

39

of the cockpit, directing the aircraft with their feet in a slewing motion, who are very much at risk of killing themselves or at least being injured if they fail to make their airfield, and fairly certain to be court-martialled if they do!

It was perhaps unsurprising that when at last the North Sea came in sight, Willis should make his remarkable suggestion:

'Why don't we head her over the sea and then bale out?'

I presumed he meant reasonably close in to the shore but as far as I was concerned the idea had no appeal. 'If we do,' I objected, 'the damn thing will probably circle round and crash on the beach or some-where. And if we haven't drowned in the process, we'll be even *worse* off then.'

Willis did not repeat the suggestion.

'We've got to get her down,' I said, looking nervously at the temperature gauge. 'And quickly!'

So we headed for the airfield, having had enough local experience by now to recognise where we were. It was only when we found it we realised that we had another problem. It was a fine day and the station was busy with trainee pilots doing their circuits and bumps – and doing them in an anti-clockwise direction. And we could only turn clockwise and only do that by dint of centralising the stick and allowing the Master to utilise its own incapacity to make the clockwise turn for us. As for the watchers below, seeing, to their astonishment, a Master breaking all the rules and regulations by doing a circuit on the wrong side of the field and in the wrong kind of orbit, they must have wondered if we had taken leave of our senses. Fortunately there was little danger of colliding head-on with another aircraft, as there was nothing to stop us making a landing in the correct direction even if we'd started from the wrong place, except that it was tricky slotting in on the penultimate easterly turn-in with other machines heading towards us westwards.

With both of us grimly hanging on to the stick and manoeuvring it into the correct position, with fabric trailing from the wings, with an engine nearly at boiling point and with little idea of our speed, we got the wheels and flaps down somehow and made a commendably correct final approach – then ruined it all by doing a double ground loop as we put her down. Why we should have executed a figure of eight I do not know – I can only presume our nerves were so ragged by now that out of the sheer relief of arriving we slackened our hold on the stick and our feet on the rudder bar.

But the undercarriage held and we taxied in to the dispersal, where our Flight Commander, Flying Officer E.W. Wooldridge, who had obviously watched the whole performance, awaited us.

We came to a halt and switched off the engine.

Wooldridge looked up at us grimly and then, having considered the damaged mainplane on his side, went to the front of the aircraft and for a moment or two disappeared from sight. When he came into view again, he had something in his hand. He held it up – a fir cone he had extracted from the radiator – and for the first time he spoke.

'You're for the high jump,' he said. 'Both of you.'

In fact he was wrong. A few days after the accident I was taken ill and carted off to Cortachy Castle, near Kirriemuir, which had been converted into a hospital. Pneumonia was diagnosed and I was put on a course of M and B – the sulpha drugs which were very new at the time. I see from my Log Book that I did no flying between 17 January and 5 March.

While away from Montrose two of my course were court-martialled: Willis and Peter Mitchell. Sharing the room at the end of the hut as we did, Mitchell had become a close friend. But he was a harum-scarum sort of chap, and one of the clearest memories I have of him is in Dundee (where we had gone on a couple of days' leave, around Christmas or New Year) listening to him, very drunk, inviting everyone who was in the bar adjacent to the ice-rink to have a drink with him.

It seemed that while I was in Cortachy Castle, Pete had done some low flying himself in a prohibited area, Balmoral I suppose – it was near enough – and been caught out. Perhaps someone read the number on his Master and reported it. Or maybe he crashed his Master. I don't know; it is too long ago to remember. Anyway a very serious view was taken and he was found guilty and condemned to ninety days in the Glasshouse – which, short of being put before a firing squad, was about the worst punishment the military could inflict. I never discovered what happened to Peter Mitchell afterwards. He was still in the Glasshouse when I finished my course at Montrose and was posted to Sutton Bridge to convert to Hurricanes.

Willis was luckier. As captain of our aircraft the responsibility for what had happened was entirely his. But the only witness to the incident was me – and I was miles away and really quite ill at the time of his court-martial. Without my evidence the prosecution was somewhat hamstrung. I don't know exactly what they charged him with but I do know that he got off with a numerically curiously coincidental fine of ninety pounds (as compared with Peter Mitchell's ninety days) which, as it represented at least a year's pay, and probably more, must have been a crushing blow to bear – but was at least better than the Glasshouse!

As for me, lucky chap – well, it was my third life and I'd got off scot-free.

PRECAUTIONARY LANDINGS

O NE of the greatest regrets of my life is that I never flew a Spitfire; one of my greatest delights that I flew Hurricanes.
The Hurricane was a wonderful aircraft, a joy to fly: robust, trustworthy and forgiving. Unlike the Master it had no malevolence. It could take punishment as could no other fighter in the world and imparted a sense of security to its pilots which I doubt if any other aircraft could match. I flew many, many hours in Hurricanes and with one single exception never had cause to doubt it. Yet, strangely, that one exception was the very first time I flew one.

It happened on 4 April 1941 at No. 56 Operational Training Unit (OTU), Sutton Bridge, which is just in Lincolnshire, being about ten miles due West of King's Lynn in Norfolk. The Commanding Officer at the time was Wing Commander Harold Maguire, who was later to end his career as Air Marshal Sir Harold Maguire, KCB, DSO, OBE. I suppose whilst at Sutton Bridge I might just have met him but I do not recollect doing so. Later I was to get to know him very well, for he was to command 266 Fighter Wing in the Dutch East Indies and we were to share harrowing experiences at the hands of the Japanese. His own exploits included bluffing the Japanese paratroops who had attacked the airfield of Palembang in Sumatra, from which we were flying at the time, into believing he had under his command a far stronger force than was in fact the case, and by this ruse managing to extricate such forces as he did have from under their very noses. This and others of his exploits I have chronicled in one of my books *Battle for Palembang*, for which he wrote the foreword. I was to share for a time the same prison camp, the native gaol of Boei Glodok in what was then Batavia, and after the war was to meet him again in England and in South Africa. He was a splendid man with splendid ideas – and if they had been accepted by the then higher command in the Far East we would, I have not the slightest doubt, have made a far better showing in Singapore, Sumatra and Java than we did.

To revert to my first flight in a Hurricane, it could not, of course, have been after instruction in flying one because a Hurricane had a single tiny cockpit and when you arrived at your Operational Training Unit you were supplied with a manual to study, and having been given half-an-hour's dual in a training aircraft (in my case in a Master) purely to familiarise you with the local geography, you were led out to a Hurricane, the layout of instruments and so on was explained and then you were told to get in and fly it!

By now of course you proudly wore your pilot's brevet, your wings, and this first solo represented a tremendous ambition realised. Yet it was a nerve-tingling moment when, with the propeller spinning and the throaty roar of a Merlin engine for the first time really in your ears, the chocks were pulled away. Here you were, a youngster whose civilian life had probably been fairly humdrum and who, if there hadn't happened to be a war would have seen the future stretching ahead in an orderly and most probably unexciting manner, who suddenly found himself a very privileged person. Here was a huge Royal Air Force Station geared only for the purpose of providing and servicing one of the world's most magnificent aircraft and presenting it to you to fly! Under your sole control was offered a machine of awe-inspiring power of whose flying capabilities you, in practical terms, knew absolutely nothing. To draw an analogy for people who have never piloted an aircraft is more than difficult – it is impossible. You could suggest the difference between, say, driving (after being instructed by your father) a pre-war Austin Seven on a private bridleway and then being told to go straight from that to driving an E-Type on a motorway. That would go some of the way towards making the point – but only some of the way. For the great distinction is that however powerful, however dynamic E-Types, Porsches, Ferraris and so on are, it is only in a two dimensional world you can drive them. They cannot soar you to the clouds or lose you in an infinity of space, and in the final analysis if they fail or their petrol runs out, dumping you miles from nowhere, you can simply open the door and walk or hitch-hike home.

It was a glorious spring day when, for the first time, I was assisted into the cockpit of Hurricane Number 1935 and the straps were placed over my shoulders and I reached for those between my legs and clipped them all home into the slots in the quick-release. I smelt for the first time that pungent smell which the cockpit of a Hurricane offers, a smell that has stayed with me all my life and is so evocative that the merest whiff of it still draws back the heavy curtain of more than sixty years and I am young again, young and eager and dis-believing I could be so fortunate.

Exactly what my instructions were on that first solo I cannot recall.

It went in the Log Book as Number 3, which is 'Effect of Controls', so I suppose we were required to fly the aircraft around the sky at will and execute a number of take-offs and landings. In my case I achieved but one of the latter, for when I made the first approach, having used the lever to lower the undercarriage, only one of the green lights came on. This could mean either that I had a faulty bulb (which was very unlikely) or that one of the oleo legs had either not come down or at least was not properly locked into place.

To land on one wheel only was not to be thought of – it would have been better to have done a belly landing with both wheels fully retracted, when the damage resulting and the risk involved would be far less. In any case neither prospect was an inviting one, and especially on my very first solo in a Hurricane, not to be considered until all alternatives had been tried.

As it happened the weather was, for early April, rather curious. We must have been in a period of high pressure, for although there was nothing which could be described as fog, or even mist, there was a definite haze to the sky which rather destroyed the horizon. With the airfield very busy with tyros like myself acclimatising themselves to flying Hurricanes, much as I had on the occasions when I got lost in fog or on that first night-flight in Montrose, I concluded that the best thing was to make myself scarce and depart from the immediate vicinity so as to be able to try, by several retractions and lowerings, to get the undercarriage properly down.

So I decided the first thing to do was to fly up above the murk. After all, one has only two hands, and it struck me there was little point in juggling between flying the aircraft partly on instruments and with the greater care which is needed when lacking a decent horizon and hoicking the undercarriage lever up and down while discussing the problem with the station below (for at last I was in an aircraft equipped with radio communication).

At about eight thousand feet I cleared the haze, and having made several fruitless attempts at getting myself two green lights, I enjoyed the brand new experience of communicating with below. Having told them of my trouble I was advised (perhaps I should have known this at the time) that it was possible to pump down a Hurricane's under-carriage by hand, that I was to try doing so but if I wasn't successful I was to do a belly-wheels-up landing. I imagine I was told where on the airfield to pick out to do this to cause the least inconvenience to all the other new pilots who were buzzing up and down like bluebottles.

Anyway, having found where the pump handle was, I followed the instructions coming from down below and eventually the green lights both came on and I descended in a rather staid fashion with wheels down through my 8,000 feet and landed without incident – my first flight having in fact taken one hour and thirty minutes, although a great deal of this was, I expect, flying around getting used to the controls before discovering I had a problem.

I can hardly rate this experience in any way as a full 'life'. With only one leg down there would have been a positive risk but with neither down one would have had to be exceptionally unlucky to be hurt. Landings by pupils who had forgotten to lower their undercarriages were common enough, but providing the landing was done on the airfield itself the only real risk involved in doing a belly landing in a Hurricane, or for that matter most monoplanes with retractable under-carriages, was that of being hauled up for a wigging and being punished in some way.

To suggest that anyone intelligent enough to have got this far in his flying training could be so thick as to forget to do something so vital as putting down his wheels may sound far-fetched, but I can assure the reader it is anything but.

To give just one example:

I was practising exercise 13 (precautionary landings) at Edzell – a satellite airfield near Montrose. Having made one landing I taxied to the take-off point but had to wait because another Master was making its landing approach. Noticing it had its wheels retracted, in an endeavour to avoid its pilot making a belly landing and all that that entailed, I deliberately taxied in front of him, forcing him to go round again. All I got for my pains as he opened the throttle and glared down at me was a shake of his fist. So when he came round again, still wheels-up, I let him have his head. He made a perfectly good landing but in doing so left his radiator a long way behind the place where he gouged to a stop, and had the nasty experience of seeing bits of his propeller whizzing past his cockpit. I believe the cost of this exercise was eight hundred pounds a go – and eight hundred pounds then was a lot of money even if it isn't nowadays.

The Master was equipped with a horn which blew if you dropped your speed below a certain level with your wheels still up, yet the number of training pilots, such as this one, who, in spite of the horn blowing raucously in their ears, landed wheels-up, was legion.

Later the pilot, whose name I have long since forgotten, apologised to me and when I asked him why he'd ignored the horn he said that he'd heard a blasted buzzing in his ears and was all set to report a fault in his machine when he got back to Montrose!

46

*　　*　　*

After completing without any remarkable incidents my course at 56 OTU I was posted to No. 3 Squadron, which at the time was based at Martlesham Heath in Suffolk. Before the war Martlesham was an experimental station at which new types of aircraft were put through their paces; after the war it was to become a light industrial centre. When my wife and I were visiting friends in Aldeburgh some years ago, I turned in through the opening to be confronted by the sight of large commercial buildings and, I believe, a police training centre or something of the sort. But I noticed that to the right of the entrance there was still some undeveloped land, and deciding to explore this, blow me down if amongst overgrown shrubs and trees I didn't find the old control tower. It put me very much in mind of Ha'penny Field: the fictional airfield of the film *The Way to the Stars*.

In that film, you may remember, an American wartime bomber pilot (played by Douglass Montgomery) goes back to his old station long after the war is over and stands nostalgically regarding his old control tower, a tattered windsock and the broken windows, et cetera, of the dispersal hut from which so many of his friends flew on missions never to return. That is how the film begins: in silence and abandonment – but then there is a roar of aircraft, the curtain of time is drawn away and we are transported back in time to a vital, throbbing wartime bomber station.

I looked for my old dispersal hut, where I had shared so much time with the other pilots of the two squadrons with which I flew at Martlesham, Numbers 3 and 258, but I did not find it. I suppose it had long since been dismantled but the control tower, unpainted, broken-windowed, untenanted, was still there and standing by it, as nostalgic as Douglas Montgomery, I could almost hear in my ears the throaty roar of Merlin engines as 'A' Flight took off on a scramble or Green Section returned from convoy patrol – could almost will Martlesham Heath to come back to wartime life like Ha'penny Field.

I loved Martlesham. It was somehow a very friendly station. Perhaps this was partly because it had no runway – for runways give an unescapable formality to an airfield. Or perhaps it was simply that it was here I served my first pleasant, untroubled days as a pilot of a fighter squadron flying Hurricanes. It's funny the things that one remembers – a fellow pilot named Gallacher with whom I was chatting one day summed up the delightful days of Martlesham. 'You know what,' he said to me, 'the one thing we've got to guard against is this war ever ending!'

Nothing much happened at Martlesham while I was there with

3 Squadron. We did innumerable convoy patrols in which the greatest danger was of drowning by ending up in the North Sea through falling asleep at the controls. We drank a lot in the evenings and we flew a lot in the days and we'd turn the oxygen full on on take-off in the (probably totally mistaken) belief that it helped ease hangovers. The convoys were very long, either convoys returning with imports or setting out to collect them. Thus they were always either northbound or southbound and were referred to by ops as either 'eggs' or 'bacon'. You couldn't possibly be confused as to which direction your convoy was heading – after all we always say north and south, not south and north don't we? And it is always eggs and bacon, isn't it? Or is it bacon and eggs?

Anyway whether north- or south-bound, or eggs or bacon, there they were and in pairs of Hurricanes from dawn to dusk we flew circuits round them at a height of 1,000 feet until our ninety minute stint was up, when we'd return to land over the fir trees which are still there lining the east side of the road from Ipswich to Woodbridge; and although we got to thinking convoy patrols were rather a bore and we weren't doing much that was useful, now and again we'd hear from someone or other how very grateful the convoys were when, as dawn came up, two Hurricanes appeared in the sky over them to protect them from marauding Dorniers or Junkers and enable them to get on with cooking their own eggs and bacon with an easier mind.

I was lucky to have been sent to Martlesham for those first days as a serving fighter pilot for, although I had not seen much of action by the time I was posted away to Kenley to join 258 Squadron with which the majority of the remainder of my flying days were to be spent, I had booked a very useful number of flying hours in my Log Book and to fly a Hurricane had become almost instinctive.

Kenley, which is near Croydon, had played a vital part in the Battle of Britain and, being close to London, was a popular station. No. 258 Squadron when I joined it had a style as different from 3 Squadron's as chalk from cheese.

One of the first things handed to me on arrival was a silver fern which I was instructed always to wear on the left breast pocket of my uniform under my brevet, for 258 had started its life as a New Zealand squadron and a silver fern is New Zealand's emblem. Time and losses had watered down the New Zealand complement but there were still, I suppose, about eight or nine Kiwis including the Commanding Officer, a dark and impressive man named Clouston, whose younger brother was also a member of the squadron. The two Flight Commanders were Kiwis as well, and both had positive personalities

Flight Lieutenant
'Denny' Sharp, who
subsequently operated
with Wingate in Burma.

and memorable features – Sharp because of his piratical appearance
and de la Perelle with a face badly scarred through bits of a cannon
shell clattering around his cockpit.

As well as New Zealanders and Limeys we had two Czechs,
Franczak and Kropiwnicki, and two more, Sticka and Sodek, who
achieved doubtful fame when the one of them who was leading their
section bellowed to the other to come into closer formation, which he
did to such effect that the bellower found his compatriot's wingtip
keeping him company in his cockpit, and the next thing we knew was
that we had two less Hurricanes in the squadron and a couple of parachutes were floating down over Purley.

We had three Poles, Zbierchowski, Paderewski and Stabrowski and
a couple of Indians, Pujji and Latif, one of whom was a Muhammadan
and the other – who wore the most beautiful of turbans held in place
by a gold brooch in the form of RAF wings – a Sikh. We had a French-
Canadian named Duval who, when shot down on one of our fighter

No 258 Squadron New Zealand pilots. *Left to right:* P/O Bruce Macalister, Flt/Lt Victor de la Perelle, Flt/Lt 'Denny' Sharp, F/O Harry Dobbyn, P/O Campbell White.

sweeps over France, achieved notoriety by launching the dinghy with which we had just been issued and which we kept packed under our parachutes, paddling back to France and then making his way into and out of Spain to return to us in triumph – only to be whisked off flying duties because a man who could do what he had done and had fluent French was clearly of more value to Intelligence.

We also had a Rhodesian, two Australians and five English making up the complement of twenty-four. Thus the squadron was a very international one and in those days when not one in a thousand youngsters had travelled any farther than Europe at best, to the handful of Britishers being part of it was an exciting experience – as was to prove our flying with it.

Fighter sweeps over France were introduced in 1941 and weather at the end of June and through the first part of July being good, we took part in them on most days. In retrospect one wonders whether fighter sweeps were, except psychologically, of real value. The format was for a couple of hundred or so Hurricanes and Spitfires to escort a small force of bombers – usually three Stirlings or a dozen Blenheims – to attack targets in such places as Lille and St Omer – the idea, we understood, being to draw up German fighters and engage with them.

Clearly because of the limited range of our fighters (two hours was very much pushing it in a Hurricane) we couldn't penetrate far into France and such a pitiful force of bombers wasn't going to trouble the Nazi war effort too much. In the Battle of Britain the advantages lay with our fighters rather than with the Germans in that we were over our home territory, and if in difficulty, able to land on one of our own many airfields or at least bale out without the problem of wondering how to escape capture by the enemy. On fighter sweeps the situation was exactly reversed. Then again there was always the question of range to be considered. This again would have been a problem to the German fighter pilots in the Battle of Britain. In our case, if, as happened frequently, you got mixed up with Me 109s or Me 110s you still had to keep a sharp eye on your petrol gauge and when the time came that, through *force majeure* you had to head for home or force-land in France or in the Channel, you were clearly at a disadvantage if there was an enemy about who had in mind attacking you.

Weighing losses of aircraft and pilots against gains, I doubt if there was much profit in the exercise but it was great for morale, and tremendous fun.

Of all the sweeps in which I took a part the one I remember best involved us rendezvousing over the Thames Estuary. We came in from the west and our job was to provide close escort above and behind the bombers, and as we turned into position I was able to scan the cloudless blue sky of yet another glorious July day and I saw from every direction, stacked up in a veritable amphitheatre, squadrons of aircraft, Hurricanes and Spitfires, all with superb timing, meeting and then in one vast wheeling operation turning to head for France. I have never forgotten that moment and the feeling of security, companionship and pride at being part of that magnificent armada.

Rarely did we manage to return to our home airfield without dropping down to refuel at one of the stations near our coastline, and this was great fun (especially if your shot-out gun ports proved you had been mixing with 109s!) Almost certainly you would bump into other pilots you'd known through your training course, who were in the same quandary as you were yourself, and over tea in the mess while they refuelled your 'kite' you would exchange experiences and 'shoot your lines'.

It was on one such occasion when for only the second time I had to contemplate putting my Hurricane down in a wheels-up landing. We had been on a sweep to Le Touquet and St Omer, and meeting some 109s had been heavy on fuel. While crossing the Channel on the way back, I realised that I would never make Kenley, and after looking in vain for an airfield at which to put down, I signalled to 'Denny' Sharp, my Flight Commander, to whom I was flying No. 2 at the time, that I'd have to put her down. He wished me luck, waved me goodbye and as I throttled back to eke out the little fuel I had left, such of the squadron as was still together was soon lost to sight.

Peering around at the patchwork fields of Kent below me for some worrying minutes, I saw nothing either sufficiently level, sufficiently treeless or of sufficient size to attract me and I had begun to fear the worst when at a distance I spotted a field which seemed large enough and level enough to be worth taking a chance on. And it certainly was. As I neared it, with flaps already down to reduce my stalling speed but wheels very firmly up, I saw to my amazement that it was teeming with Hurricanes and Spitfires, like bees around a honeypot. How lucky could you be – for my field was none other than West Malling airfield!

It was a bit of a bother getting down with everyone in the same boat, all but dry, and, with nobody willing to yield a yard on the approach, we were landing almost in formation. But all went well and there were old friends who had been posted to other stations to chat with, and strawberries and cream for tea.

It is perhaps stretching it a bit to claim these Sutton Bridge and West Malling experiences as, even taken together, constituting a life, but there was certainly in both cases luck involved – and luck, after all, was, above everything else, what a wartime fighter pilot's life depended on.

TORA! TORA! TORA!

O N 10 July 1941 258 Squadron took over from 3 Squadron at Martlesham Heath, the decision no doubt having been taken to give its pilots a rest after the busy period they had known and the significant losses they had suffered whilst flying from Kenley. Through the next twelve weeks or so there was a great deal of flying done – largely on convoy patrols but with diversions such as occasional scrambles or air-sea rescue patrols searching for pilots who had been shot down or had force-landed in the North Sea.

On 1 October the squadron, having been posted overseas, flew to Debden to obtain experience in flying Hurricanes fitted with cannons and long-range tanks prior to being shipped to Gibraltar, whence it was to board the aircraft carrier *Ark Royal*, fly off her deck to Luqa in Malta and thence to Alexandria. Its intended role (to be shared with two other Hurricane squadrons, 242 and 605) was tank-busting in the desert in Operation Crusader, which was intended to sweep Rommel from Cyrenaica.

By now 258's complement was vastly changed. We no longer had any Czechs, Poles or Indians and only five New Zealanders remained, the deficit being made up by two new Canadians, five Americans and the balance Britishers. But the greatest change of all was the loss of Squadron Leader Clouston, who had been posted out to Singapore, and his replacement by a new Commanding Officer, Squadron. Leader Thomson. But we still wore our New Zealand ferns, indulged at the slightest opportunity in singing with actions the squadron song 'To you sweetheart, Aloha', and on important occasions such as embarkation leave, the few remaining Kiwis entertained us, and admiring and surprised spectators, with a rousing haka.

When I reported at Uxbridge (having volunteered to join the Royal Air Force because my brother was already in it) I found myself in a very long queue in a very long and very broad hut. After an hour or so of inching along towards the Recruiting Officer's room, a man a couple ahead of me stopped a passing orderly to enquire what the very

No. 258 Squadron pilots at Debden prior to embarkation. *Left to right, front row:* P/O Fletcher, P/O Geffene, P/O Nash, P/O Macnamara, F/O Dobbyn, Flt/Lt Sharp, S/Ldr Thomson, G/C Churchill, unknown, Flt/Lt de la Perelle, P/O Macalister, P/O White, P/O Kleckner, P/O McCulloch, P/O Milnes, P/O Cicurel. *Back row:* P/O Campbell, unknown, Sgt Pilots: Lambert, Sheerin, Healey, Gallacher, Scott, Kelly, Keedwell, Miller, Nichols, Glynn, unknown. G/C Churchill, the officer on his left, Sgt Pilot Gallacher and the unknowns did not accompany the squadron overseas. A fifth American, F/O Donahue, also joined and accompanied the squadron. The only pilots not killed or taken prisoner by the Japanese were: Macnamara, Sharp, Thomson, White, McCulloch, Milnes, Sheerin, Miller and Nichols.

short queue (never more than three or four) across the corridor from us, was about.

'That? Oh, that's to join the Navy,' the orderly replied.

'Well, bugger this for a lark,' (or something equivalent) the disgruntled volunteer replied, quit us and tagged himself on the end of this opposite queue. And a few minutes later he was waving us goodbye with a: 'Cheerio, chaps, I'm in the Navy.'

I have often wondered what happened to that fellow. Did he become an Admiral or was he depth-charged in a submarine? Did he spend the war afloat or clerking in some shore establishment? Who knows? One thing is certain: by the impatience which led to that hasty decision not only his own life but undoubtedly the lives of scores, perhaps

The American and Canadian pilots in 258 Squadron. *Left to right:* Sgt Keedwell, P/O Cicurel, P/O Geffene, P/O Kleckner, P/O Campbell, Sgt Miller, Sgt Scott. The only pilot not killed or taken prisoner by the Japanese was Sgt Miller.

hundreds, of other men and women would have been quite changed – for everything we do has that ripple effect.

In the case of the twenty-four pilots of 258 Squadron it was the mere toss of coins which utterly changed their lives. *Ark Royal* could accommodate only thirty-six Hurricanes additional to her normal complement of aircraft, and coins were spun to decide which thirty-six of the seventy-two pilots should be in the first batch to fly off her to Malta. The upshot of the coin-tossing was that 258 and half of 605 Squadron remained in Gibraltar while *Ark Royal* steamed off to launch 242 and the other half of 605 at Point X, somewhere in the Mediterranean. On her way back to collect 258 and the balance of 605's pilots, *Ark Royal* was sunk, and while the powers who decide these things were wondering what on earth to do with thirty-six Hurricane pilots marooned on Gibraltar, Japan, by declaring war, supplied the answer: 'Send them to Singapore!' – a decision which delighted our five Americans, livid over Japan's dastardly attack on Pearl Harbor.

Making our way there was full of incident and interest, but as I have

No. 258 Squadron pilots at Port Sudan.

already chronicled it in detail in my book *Hurricane Over the Jungle*, I will only paraphrase it now.

We reboarded the ship which had delivered us to Gibraltar from Greenock, HMS *Athene*, and sailed on her to Takoradi on the Gold Coast. From the RAF station there we boarded a Douglas DC-3 and flew across Africa to Wadi Saidna (near Kharthoum) landing *en route* at Accra on the Gold Coast, at Lagos, Kano and Maiduguri in Nigeria, and El Fasher in Sudan. From. Kharthoum we flew to Port Sudan where we taxied Hurricanes equipped with long-range tanks down to the dockside, where they were loaded on HMS *Indomitable* (a brand new aircraft carrier making her maiden operational voyage), from which we, and twenty-four pilots of 232 Squadron (who had made a similar trip to ours across Africa) flew off at a point near the Chagos Archipelago to Kemajoran Airport in Jakarta, then called Batavia, capital of Java. Of the forty-eight Hurricanes which took off from *Indomitable* forty-seven reached Java, the forty-eighth having landed back on *Indomitable* when its pilot diagnosed engine trouble on take-off. This, incidentally, was a remarkable performance executed by a not very experienced pilot of 232 Squadron. We had been instructed before take-off that in the event of any difficulty arising we were not, repeat not, to attempt to land back on the carrier as this could not be done successfully by Hurricanes not equipped with arrester gear. However, the pilot in question, taking a poor view of his chances if he did what he had been ordered to do – ditch in the ocean – succeeded in the impossible, and after the inevitable wigging for disobeying orders, was rewarded with a model of *Indomitable* specially commissioned for him and made aboard the ship. He would have been highly delighted with his prize and no doubt considered he had made a wise choice; had he known what lay ahead for the remaining twenty-three pilots of his squadron he would have been even more certain of it.

From Kemajoran we flew in penny numbers up to Singapore via Palembang in Sumatra. The first eight Hurricanes of 258 Squadron became operational on 1 February 1942 and (meeting a vastly superior force of Zeros flown by very experienced Japanese pilots) 258 scored its first successes and suffered its first casualties. After a few days of mixed fortunes in the air and being bombed and machine-gunned on the ground, the squadron was ordered back to Palembang, where fate kindly granted me my fifth life.

While flying in the UK, over France and in the Far East there could not, I think, have been many 258 Squadron pilots who were not engaged at some time or other in aerial combat. But as, after all, that is what any wartime fighter pilot would expect, what in fact being a fighter pilot was in the main all about, although these incidents may be referred to, to provide context and background, I am not including any such engagements in which I or other pilots were involved, as constituting lives. A life for the purpose of this book is an incident, perhaps prolonged, where good fortune, perhaps sometimes better called good luck, attended me personally and where I came through a dangerous (or at least risky) situation unscathed. So far as these occurred in the Far East theatre, surviving fellow pilots of 258, 232 and 605 Squadrons, and of other squadrons such as 242 and 488 New Zealand Squadron who flew in the area, could, I am quite sure, had they put pen to paper, have easily matched them, for although of comparatively short duration it was a period of intense activity and of grievous losses in air crew.

Not that the chances of being killed were limited to encounters in the air. The Japanese were very conscious that success in their drive southwards very much depended on air superiority, and it followed that the places where pilots were most likely to be found – on airfields – were prime targets for attack.

Our first personal experience of this sort of thing was in Singapore. Much has been written about the Japanese bombing of Singapore and it has been cited time and time again as one of the principal reasons for the island's fall. Such claims are arrant nonsense – as was the claim I had to listen to recently on a trip to Japan with other ex-Japanese prisoners of war, which was made by a Singaporean to an audience of schoolchildren of many nationalities that the reason for the island's fall was 'not because the defenders were in any way inferior as soldiers but because we had no aircraft.'

When, in some choler, I interrupted to ask him to explain, if this were so, the fact that, for example, 232 Squadron, flying Hurricanes, lost more than half its pilots, killed within nine days of their arrival in Singapore, he answered, testily:

'Well, all right . . .' and immediately went on as if I had not posed the question: 'From my own experience the only British aircraft I saw were squadrons of Hurricanes which escorted Wavell on his last visit to the island. You will find this is the general impression from Singapore people from their own experience.'

The principal reasons for the fall of Singapore were appalling leadership and the bust morale which was probably inevitable after the endless withdrawals from one place after another all the way down the Malay Peninsula. To say this is not to denigrate those who were taken prisoner on the island. They were after all just as much a cross-section of Allied troops as were those who fought the Japanese in Burma and threw them out.

Nor can it be denied that the fact that the Japanese had air superiority over the skies of Singapore and appeared to be able to bomb the island at will must have been a contributory factor in the loss of morale amongst the troops, and for that matter RAF groundstaff, but to ascribe the loss of Singapore to this is quite absurd. The Japanese, after all, held out for far longer periods, against far greater odds and under the pressure of far heavier bombing on island after island in the Pacific before the Americans finally recaptured them.

In any case, whilst the Japanese did bomb Singapore, and bombed it regularly, by the standards of war in other theatres, especially later, the bombing was very light. Almost without exception it was carried out in the mornings only, sometimes in one raid, sometimes in two – never, so far as I know, in more. The targets were the four airfields of Tengah, Seletar, Kallang and Sembawang, the docks, and the town itself, and the bombing was carried out by flights of twenty-seven bombers flying in perfect Hendon Air Display formations. The process of dropping their bombs (often clusters of 40 pound anti-personnel bombs) was effected by all being dropped together on the instruction of the flight leader. Except when the town itself was attacked, casualties were minimal. If not flying, we would stand, perhaps with a glass of beer in hand, watching these formations approaching (never more than two formations of twenty-seven, usually only one, and always protected by a screen of fighters of, I suppose, roughly similar numbers) and forecast from their direction which was this group's likely target. If we judged it to be our own airfield we would move to the edge of one of the slit trenches (about two feet wide and six or so feet deep) and wait, watching. As the bombs were released you could hear the whistle of their falling and there was time enough to put your glass unhurriedly by the edge of the trench, get down into it and wait for the longish extended 'crrrumph' of the bombs exploding and then get out again, recover your beer and watch the formations turning round to fly back to their captured Malayan bases. Army and RAF personnel were, of course, sometimes killed or wounded in these attacks, but casualties were very few in number, and your personal risk if handy to a slit trench was microscopic.

There is, however, another form of attack by enemy aircraft which is far more personal and was in our case far more dangerous – and that

Servicing aircraft at P.2, Sumatra.

is ground-strafing. This I was to experience in both Sumatra and Java and, ironically, also as a prisoner in Japan from aircraft from, of all ships, HMS *Indomitable*!

In Palembang, Sumatra, while operating from the KLM civilian airport (which we dubbed P.1 to distinguish it from a huge jungle airfield some forty or so miles to the south which we dubbed P.2.), we had our first tastes of this unpleasant business, and if the first occasion was not, in terms of pilots and groundstaff lost and damage inflicted, the most serious, it was, I have always felt, the most dramatic.

On orders we had withdrawn that morning from Tengah airfield in Singapore, landing well ahead of the torrential rain which almost invariably fell for much of the afternoon. This was, I suppose, with Singapore having a similar climate to Sumatra, the probable reason for the rarity of Japanese afternoon attacks there.

The downpour having at last ceased, relaxing after the stress of Singapore, vainly imagining that the Japanese would hardly bother us with their hands being full subduing the island, we were sitting comfortably in chairs on the verandah of the terminal building, smoking, chatting and viewing above us a sky which was still as black as thunder. The sound of approaching aircraft surprised us but, greatly impressed that in spite of such filthy weather conditions this reinforcement should have found P.1 at all, we assumed it was more Hurricanes arriving from Java as the practice was to send up batches as soon as a few had been made ready for combat duty.

It was the normal practice of a fighter squadron when arriving at a new station to beat it up in formation before climbing away, breaking up into pairs or single aircraft and landing. And so when out of a very small gap in the clouds directly ahead of us we saw the distant dots of a flight of small and obviously single-engined aircraft, emerging and heading towards us in a dive, we sat back comfortably to enjoy the performance. It was only when they were near enough for us to see that they had radial rather than in-line engines that we realised that these were not Hurricanes but Zeros – or Navy 0s as we called them at the time.

P.1 had two runways, one running the full length of the airfield, the other (which was much shorter) crossing it at an angle. The main runway ran north and south and pointed directly at the terminal building in front of which we were sitting, and it was along the length of this runway, or parallel to it, that the Navy 0s were making their attack, and we had scarcely jumped to our feet before the air was filled with the whine of bullets and cannon shells, the shattering of glass and the roar of the first of the Zeros passing only feet above our heads as

The Japanese fighter known to the first pilots who met it as the Navy 0 or the Navy Nought, later dubbed the Zero.

they pulled out of their dives to climb, circle and return to attack again.

Through the miracle of sight, we have presented to us through our lifetime a stream of images which only sleep or the closing of our eyes interrupts. It is as though the brain is a ciné-camera and our eyes the lenses through which it observes the ever-changing prospect which is entirely personal to us. If each second of sight could be represented by one single image of a movie film, through an average lifetime the brain would observe and react to some two and a half thousand million images, and by another miracle, store an astounding number of them. Even more amazing is its ability, when prompted, perhaps, by something very modest such as a casual remark, a waft of perfume or a snatch of melody, to at once extract from all these millions of stored images and present to our consciousness one or a series which takes us back in time as if the happening were only yesterday.

Sometimes we are surprised by the clarity with which a past happening – which until that moment we had perhaps even forgotten had occurred – is presented; conversely there are images so deeply imprinted in our beings that we do not need the medium of reminders to call them to view. And in my own case this latter consideration applies to the happenings of that afternoon in February 1942.

As I sit here now I can see those tiny dots emerging from a rift in a sky of overlapping slates; I can see those radial engines bearing down on us across the width of what, little changed, is now once again Palembang's commercial airport; and, clearest of all, I can see the

61

blood red circles of the Japanese insignia on the wings of a Navy 0 almost, it seems, within touching distance of my head as it roars upwards climbing above the roof of the terminal building.

There was at once action and confusion on that jungle airfield. Amongst our little group the pilots on readiness that afternoon, all miraculously unhurt, were hastily grabbing at essentials and racing to their aircraft, and groundstaff were running to help them in and start them up. Others, with no purpose in remaining as target practice, were running for the doubtful cover of the jungle. A few feet away from me, almost close enough for me to touch him, a man was shrieking and clutching at his stomach. More Navy 0s were attacking, and one of our Americans, Red Campbell, had hauled his revolver out and was taking pot shots at them. Our airfield Bofors guns were firing, 'cudumph, cudumph, cudumph'. The first Hurricanes were taxying fast, wheeling and tearing down the runway to do battle. Soon the chatter of Brownings was intermingled with the spatter of the Japanese machine guns and the pop of cannons. As the mayhem of the attack itself died down there were air battles to witness against the background of the heavy cloud: a Japanese fighter hurtling earthwards into the jungle, a Hurricane with a Zero on its tail with the white of glycol streaming from it. And then it was over: the Japanese fighters heading home; the few Hurricanes which had managed to get airborne landing, mostly at P.2.

Strangely the attack had been almost a total failure. No Hurricanes on the ground had been damaged; none in the air shot down. The only casualties had been amongst the groundstaff.

It was only when I went back to the verandah of the terminal building that I realised quite how lucky we, the pilots of 258 Squadron, had been, and myself especially, for there was a bullet hole through one of the chromium-plated legs of the chair on which I had been sitting; and the glass panel just to my left on which the readiness situation (the names of the pilots due to fly that afternoon) had been chalked lay in shattered pieces on the floor!

There was, however, one consequence of the attack which for all the drama of the event caused a chuckle or two amongst the pilots who had been in the terminal building when it was made. On the wall behind us there hung a splendid picture of a line of British battleships, White Ensigns proudly flying. By the time the Navy 0s had finished with us, this impressive piece of propaganda was hanging at a drunken angle threatening to hit the floor at any instant. This would not have mattered all that much but for its caption: 'The downfall of the dictators is assured.'

*   *   *

What had been a new experience was to be repeated frequently. On the very next day the Japanese again attacked P.1 in a far more effective raid in which bombers as well as fighters were involved. By the end of the day three of our pilots were dead and one was dying. Two were missing and three more had had their machines badly shot about, and their pilots had either baled out or crash-landed in the jungle. It was only in the evening that we were able accurately to assess our losses. We met for dinner in the restaurant at the Luxor Cinema in the town, arriving in dribs and drabs – for some of those flying had landed back at P.1, others at P.2. As each man arrived his name was added to the list. When, after a longish gap, there were no more arrivals we knew the score and sat down to eat.

Later, in Java, when there were only four of us out of the original twenty-four of 258 Squadron still flying, we were to be given much the same sort of treatment by the Japanese at Tjillillitan airfield in Batavia. At the time Tjillillitan was a military airfield; now it is the civilian airport serving Jakarta, and is called Perdanakusama after a leading revolutionary in the Indonesian fight for independence from the Dutch. When my wife accompanied me on a nostalgic return to these parts of the world, it was where we landed. From it we flew up to Palembang and landed at P.1. It was a strange feeling returning to these two airfields where such dramatic happenings took place and so many who had become close friends were killed. Now they have all the dressings of modern airfields and there is absolutely nothing to give the slightest clue that once, for a very brief period, they were the principal targets of the Japanese invaders. Seeing them humming with life, teeming with travellers, of whom the vast majority were Indonesians, one felt curiously alone. One wanted to touch one of them on the arm and say: 'Look! See there! That's where one of our Americans, a man named Kleckner who came from Texas, stopped General Wavell, who had landed *en route* from Singapore to Australia, and told him why we were going to lose Singapore, what we should have done in Singapore and where we went wrong in Singapore.' Cardell Kleckner – who the very next day was to be shot down and killed.

And at Perdanakusama? Was there the same temptation there? No, not at Perdanakusama. P.1 has retained the character we knew. You can still look at the jungle bordering the end of the runway and see those Navy 0s we thought were Hurricanes diving down. But Perdanakusama is just another civilian airport – huge, impersonal and without a soul.

*   *   *

As if they could not bear to leave us alone, having come to the end of our flying days we were to be treated to a final strafing by the Japanese.

Although by now we had no Hurricanes to fly, the Dutch authorities dithered while there was still time for us to have got away from Java and use our hard-won battle experience at first in Sri Lanka (then Ceylon) and later in Burma. Too late they gave approval, and to meet a sailing deadline we drove in a hair-raising moonlit journey to the southern port of Tjilatjap to catch a ship which would take us to freedom. But there was no ship. Perhaps it had sailed a few hours before our arrival – perhaps there hadn't been one at all. We were never to find out.

We crashed out in a small hotel and the next morning with the Japanese already ashore in several places in the north of Java and a thousand or more miles of ocean between us and freedom, we were knocking back champagne and trying to decide what to do when the Japanese attacked Tjilatjap. Why on earth they attacked it I do not know; perhaps it was an attack pencilled in before they realised that Java would fall almost without a fight.

Whatever the reason they made a good job of it with flights of dive-bombers. We scuttled out of the hotel into a nullah (drain) across the road – it was just like old times in Singapore. When the attack was over we returned to the hotel. On the champagne in the glasses we had left unfinished were thick layers of plaster from the ceiling. So we opened new bottles. The proprietor didn't mind – he'd read the writing on the wall.

Many years later, on my return trip to Indonesia, my wife and I drove to Tjilatjap. I didn't imagine we would find that hotel; I didn't know where it was, what street it was in. But as we drove into the town Ann, pointing, said: 'You know that could have been a hotel.' I stopped the car. 'No,' I said. 'Our hotel had a deep drain just across the road from it. There isn't one here.' But there happened to be a Dutch-man passing by – which was odd because by then most of the Dutch had quitted Java. So we asked him. 'Yes,' he said. 'That used to be a hotel.'

'But there isn't a drain!'

'Well there is, you know,' he said. 'But they've covered it up.'

And we went across the road and, sure enough, there was the drain in which we'd sheltered from that final strafing.

But why head this chapter Tora! Tora! Tora!?

There was a film made in America covering the Japanese attack on

64

TORA! TORA! TORA!

Pearl Harbor. Its title was *Tora! Tora! Tora!* While I wouldn't stake my life on it, from recollection these were the words the Japanese pilots carrying out their dive-bombing and strafing were shouting gleefully as they attacked. I can well imagine them shouting 'Tora! Tora! Tora!' as they strafed us on P.1, at Tjillillitan and at Tjilatjap.

SIXTH LIFE

CLOSE QUARTERS

PRESUMABLY because no one on *Indomitable* had any knowledge of the capabilities of Japanese fighters and their pilots, we had no briefing on them while on board and when we flew off her, eager to get into action, we were confident that with our splendid Hurricanes we would soon be sweeping the skies over Malaya and Singapore clean of these strange characters and their wooden biplanes.

I was initially tempted to write that the discovery that, far from being held together with string, the Navy 0 (or Zero) was a very good fighter which had many advantages over the Hurricane came as a shock. But on thinking it over I realised that that would have been inaccurate. We were not thrown into either confusion or dismay – but we were certainly surprised, furious that we had not been properly briefed and only too conscious that a learning process had to be gone through before we could find the way to utilise effectively the definite advantages the Hurricane possessed in combat.

These can be briefly stated: firstly, the Hurricane with twelve machine-guns (later, to improve manoeuvrability, reduced in many machines to eight) had a better firepower than the Navy 0, with its twin cannons and machine-guns; secondly, being a wonderfully sturdy aircraft it could accept punishment which would have scattered the flimsier Navy 0 to pieces; finally, it was capable of flying at a higher altitude than the Navy 0 could reach. So far as top speeds and rate of climb were concerned I do not believe there was very much in it and I would not now hazard a guess as to whether or not one had the edge over the other, but in certain aspects the Navy 0 had very positive advantages, the most important of these being that it was distinctly more manoeuvrable.

Having been led to believe that the Hurricane was the most manoeuvrable modern fighter aircraft (which in Europe it certainly was) and no one on *Indomitable*, in Java or in Sumatra on our way up to Singapore having disabused us, even when we were informed in hushed, awed terms of the Navy 0's potentiality by the groundstaff who were there to service us on the island, we did not for a moment imagine it could out-turn us. And so, while going through the learning process we lost pilots quickly.

Even so, I do not recall that even the loss of a quarter of our twenty-four pilots within eight days of flying off *Indomitable* affected the morale of the survivors. We were experiencing the most hectic and exciting times of our lives, with every day filled with incident from dawn to dusk. Then, again, our evenings were spent in an atmosphere utterly foreign to anything we had even imagined previously, and through each one we secretly gave thanks for the fact that we were still alive, and within the limitations that Singapore and Palembang imposed, set about enjoying the free hours to the full. Tomorrow would be another day and with a bit of luck, and by incorporating the lessons learnt from this day's disasters into tomorrow's tactics, we would find the way to mix it with Zeros and survive.

This is not to say that there were any of us who were not perfectly conscious that tomorrow might be the last day on earth for some of us – at the Luxor restaurant in Palembang tomorrow, after the roll call had been taken, we might well be raising our glasses to Rupert, shot down that morning or Christopher (the names are fictitious), caught by machine-gun fire while running to his kite.

For this was how we saw our possible deaths: whether in the sky or

Hurricanes taxying to stern of aircraft carrier *Indomitable.*

on the ground, always at the hands of enemy aircraft. It never crossed our minds that we could be at risk of meeting the Japanese at closer quarters.

One of the special advantages of choosing to be aircrew in the war was the element of detachment which soldiers never knew – an element which, perhaps, was shared by those who were in the Navy and afloat. Our business was flying and once we'd quit our aircraft and left the airfield we were basically done with playing any part in the war until we climbed back into a cockpit again.

Or so we thought.

The events of 14 February 1942 (the day before Singapore fell to the Japanese) were to prove how very wrong we could be.

Oddly enough it was the day on which we were able to put the largest number of Hurricanes into the air together – fourteen, no less! It will be remembered that forty-eight had flown off *Indomitable* and forty-seven had arrived in Java. Wastage began immediately. Faulty brakes caused losses at Kemajoran Airport on arrival while others, landing across deep ruts left by transiting Flying Fortresses at P.2, had their undercarriages collapse under them. Some were shot from the skies over Singapore or Sumatra, some destroyed on the ground and some pilots had to make forced landings in the strangest of places when engine or other troubles developed. Then again, the absurd decision to send Hurricanes up to the war theatres in penny numbers as soon as they had been serviced and pronounced airworthy resulted in such as were available being split between Singapore, Sumatra and Java.

So by comparison with earlier days, fourteen looked, as we taxied out preparatory to taking off from P.1, impressive. Our mission was to escort a force of bombers detailed to attack an enemy convoy in the Banka Straits – a stretch of water between the east coast of Sumatra and the large island of Banka. The idea was that we would wait on the ground with engines ticking over until the Blenheims, presumably flying from P.2, arrived overhead, and then take off. After a while, when the Blenheims didn't show, our CO, Thomson, decided we wouldn't wait any longer. Maybe he had good reasons, but personally I have never been able to understand the thinking. We did not at the time have the least notion that invasion of Sumatra was imminent and we hadn't the slightest knowledge of what the convoy comprised or even exactly where it was. If we had found it I don't know exactly what, without bombs or even cannons, we could have done to hinder it; spraying ships with machine-guns was hardly the most effective use of our meagre resources.

Anyway we took off and headed vaguely towards Banka Island. We

RAF Lockheed Hudsons.

were heartened *en route* by the sight of a large formation of Lockheed
Hudsons heading in the opposite direction and passing just below us
half-shielded from our sight by a thin skein of cloud. In fact these
were not friendly aircraft but Japanese aircraft carrying paratroops.
There were, according to the Japanese records, forty of them and they
were a mixture of Lockheeds bought from the Lockheed Corporation
or made under licence and Japanese-made Kawasaki Ki-57s which
were almost identical in appearance to Lockheeds, and no doubt, were
simple copies of them. In retrospect it has always been surprising to
me that for all that veil of cloud not one of the fourteen of us looking
down on that formation spotted the red Japanese roundels on their
wings. There are those who say they had fake British markings but
somehow I doubt it. It also seems very strange that Thomson didn't
mentally enquire how on earth a formation of our own aircraft could
be heading from that direction towards Palembang (when we all knew
that they couldn't have come from Singapore, which was by now prac-
tically speaking, devoid of Allied bombers) and why he didn't take the
time to do a circuit, or at least detach a couple of us to investigate. We
continued blithely on our way to look for the convoy – which we never
found – while the Lockheeds flew to P.1 and dropped their paratroops.

At this distance it all sounds very foolish but it is only fair to

Thomson to point out that such information as we received from ground command was usually sketchy and often incorrect, that radio communication was usually poor and often non-existent (I, myself, and at least one other pilot had none at all that day), and that our mission was a precise one: to escort some bombers which, as they hadn't shown over P.1 were, presumably, somewhere about, heading for Banka and wondering what had happened to their fighter escort.

We were returning from our fruitless flight to an airfield surrounded by jungle (in which, although we did not yet know it, there were now several hundred Japanese paratroops) when to my surprise Thomson abruptly changed direction, taking a far more southerly course, and the whole formation wheeled to stay with him. As I was to learn later this was obeying an order that we were not to land at P.1 because of the paratroops but to proceed instead to P.2 – but as I didn't have a functioning radio in my own Hurricane I was merely puzzled and, looking about me, I discovered what I thought at first was the reason: a collection of Navy 0s above us. But as the formation continued serenely on in its new direction, I realised that no one else had spotted them, and being unable to communicate by radio, I broke formation, went to the head of it and furiously waggled my wings and pointed upwards. Even after all these years I can see Thomson barking into his transmitter and when this had no effect, gesticulating at me angrily to get back into formation. Something had to be done even if I was the only one to do it – fortunately I wasn't. One other pilot, Bertie Lambert, had also seen the Navy 0s and joined with me in trying to do something about them.

Meanwhile the balance of the squadron, amazingly unmolested by the Navy 0s, carried on towards P.2, which it reached without alarm.

So far as I was concerned, however, the next half an hour or so was anything but without incident. In the course of it I was involved in aerial combat and ended up being chased by a Navy 0 which at a low altitude got nicely on my tail. Now I was in a fix. If I'd tried to climb away he would have got me on the climb and if I'd turned he'd have got me on the turn. The only escape was ignominious flight down to treetop level in the hope I could somehow shake him off. So down I went, skidding a ragged course using rudder more than aileron. If I had thought about it at the time I would have blessed Wilson for obliging me to commit near-suicide in our absurdly reckless low-flying exploits at Montrose; without that experience I could never have got away with it. Of course it wasn't easy for the Jap in that Zero. His own line of sight would always have been impeded by the body and wings of his own aircraft. If he'd tried climbing a little prior to diving down on me again, he might have lost me, and anyway, because you have to allow for deflection in diving down he would have had to shoot a little ahead of me for me to run into his bullets or cannon shells, and he couldn't do that because his own wings would have hidden me (and the trees he was in danger of hitting) from sight. And the same sort of consideration would have applied if he'd tried to get me on a turn. And of course he didn't want to hit the trees any more than I did. So it went on for quite a little while, and in the process of the chase (to the astonishment – as I was to hear later – of ground staff who saw a Hurricane appear from nowhere at nought feet, hotly pursued by a Navy 0) we cleared the town of Palembang and went back over the jungle. Now and then I caught a glimpse of him in my mirror and then, of a sudden, he was gone. Maybe he hit a tree, or maybe he got fed up or got worried about how much petrol he had left and headed home. Who knows?

By now in a terrible muck sweat but mightily relieved, I set course back to, as I thought, the comparative calm and safety of P.1, hoping that by the time I got there all the other Navy 0s would have gone home as well.

In fact they had, and with much relief I made a normal circuit and landed on the runway, turning at its end where another Hurricane had come to a sticky end the previous day . Its pilot, a man named Parr, had had a finger shot off on the throttle which jammed open and forced him to come in to land too fast and then, with nice judgement, switch off the engine and come in at least slow enough not to kill himself or completely write off the Hurricane. I had gone out with others in a Commer to pick him up, and he had pulled out the finger, which he had apparently put into his pocket, held it up and said 'I guess I won't be needing this any more!' It is a pity we didn't know the things that we know now or we might have told him to stick it on again, or perhaps he did know and did stick it on. I couldn't say. I never saw Dicky Parr again after that occasion – things were too busy.

Anyway his machine had been shoved a little aside and wasn't in the way, and I taxied back along the runway to the spot where I normally parked my Hurricane, expecting to see a bowser already motoring out to fill me up with petrol – for it was essential that this should be done the moment a Hurricane landed, in case of a surprise attack. But not only was there no sign of any bowser moving but there were no groundstaff running out to help me down, no armourers to reload the guns and no crew to cover the gunports which had, of course, been shot away, check the glycol and all the rest of it.

It was very odd.

I undid my straps, unclasped my parachute harness, leaving it in the bucket seat, turned the gun button, which I had forgotten, away from 'Fire', put my helmet over the gunsight, stripped my gauntlets off, hauled myself out of the cockpit, felt for and found the step in the fuselage and jumped down to the ground.

I couldn't but feel frustrated. I had had a very exciting hour or more – in fact my Log Book says one hour and forty minutes, which is getting near to a Hurricane's range limit – and I had shot down a Navy 0 and been chased all over Palembang and I was agog to tell everyone about it.

But there was no one to tell it to. No one. The airfield was utterly deserted.

I remembered how, a few years earlier, I had read the story of *Beau Geste* (or perhaps I'd seen the film) and there was this scene where a relieving force arrives at a desert fort to find the tables laid for a meal but not a soul in the fort to eat it. Not a sound broke the silence. An empty fort in an empty desert – and utter silence.

Well, that was exactly how it was at P.1 as I quit my Hurricane and stood bewildered and alone. The best part of two hours before I had taken off from a bustling airfield and now I was back on it and everything was exactly as it had been: the unserviceable Hurricanes were parked where they had been parked before, the petrol bowsers were in sight, as were the starter batteries and all the other bits and pieces and paraphernalia which are always present on a busy fighter airfield. The airport building was unchanged, glittering in the sunshine, and the chairs we sat in (even mine with the bullet hole through the leg) were ranged on the verandah in front of it. And all around was the ever-present jungle. All was exactly as it had been before I took off nearly two hours before – all except the people and the sound of them.

I have no idea what I would have done had it not been that at that moment I heard an aircraft approaching and I knew it was a Hurricane because the sound of the Merlin engine is unmistakable. I knew the tanks in my own Hurricane must be very nearly empty – the question of taking off again and trying to reach P.2 did not seem to arise. And in any case, apart from the silence and emptiness around me, I couldn't begin to guess the answer to this mystery.

With considerable relief I watched the Hurricane making its absolutely normal and unhurried circuit of the field, cross it at the southern boundary over my head, land on the runway, turn by Parr's machine, taxi back towards where I was standing and draw up beside my own machine.

Switching off the engine and doing all the things which I had done a few minutes earlier, the pilot got out and joined me.

It was Bertie Lambert. He glanced around, amazed.

'What's going on, Terry?'

'You tell me.'

'Where the hell is everybody?'

'I haven't a clue. You didn't hear anything on your R/T?'

'Duff.'

'So's mine.'

'Where's the rest of them?' Meaning 258 pilots.

'Gone to P.2, I suppose. They were heading that way when I tried to show Thomson there were Navy 0s about. You saw them, Bertie? That was you came up with me, wasn't it?'

'It certainly was.'

'Get any?'

Bertie nodded. 'Yes. I got one. You do any good?'

'Got a Navy 0. And got chased all over the place by another one.'

But what we'd done or what had happened to us was not the important thing – the important thing was to find out what had happened on P.1 and discover what we were supposed to do: two pilots with all but dry Hurricanes on an abandoned airfield.

But just then a man burst from the jungle which shrouded the airfield's edge: 'Micky' Nash – one of 258's pilots who'd been acting as Duty Officer that morning.

He came running up to us, breathless and disbelieving.

'What the hell are you doing here? Didn't you get the gen on your R/T?'

'Duff,' we repeated.

'Well you can't walk out and you can't drive out, there's Jap paratroops all around the place. Hundreds of the bastards! You must have crossed right over them coming in.'

I remembered the Lockheed Hudsons.

'Only kites I saw were Lockheeds . . .'

'Packed with bloody paratroops!'

'Good God!' I said. And, after a moment, 'They must have had British markings. If they had those poached eggs we'd have seen them. Wouldn't we?'

But I wasn't sure. There had been that skein of cloud.

'You know what,' Bertie said. 'They were definitely Lockheed Hudsons. You couldn't be wrong about those trailing flaps. You know what – I bet the blighters bought them from the Yanks.' And, at a thought, 'My God, what a beano we could have had!'

But Nash spoke grimly. 'You've got one now. Listen!'

We listened and for the first time heard rifle fire. I have often thought how strange it was that we could have stood, if only for a minute or so, talking and heard no sound of warfare. I suppose one and then a second Hurricane unexpectedly coming into land had momentarily stilled both the Japanese and our own people.

'You're lucky,' Nash (who now that Glynn had been killed was the youngest of the 258 Squadron pilots – still only twenty, I believe) said enviously, 'you've got kites.'

'If they start,' said Bertie.

'And if they've got enough juice left, Mine's showing s.f.a.'

'Mine too.'

'Well, you'd better make your minds up.' And at a sudden thumping sound, 'or take your chance in there.' He was pointing to the jungle.

'That was mortars, wasn't it?' said Bertie, solemnly.

'Hand grenades,' said Micky, now a man of some experience.

'What are you going to do, Micky?'

'Get the hell out of sight before they start shooting at us.'

I didn't like the look of the green jungle and nor did Bertie, but in a squadron there was form to things.

'But, Micky . . .'

'For God's sake! If you aren't quick, you won't get started.'

A Hurricane's engine was usually started by means of a starter battery whose lead was plugged in. But so long as the engine was warm enough, with luck one could manage without.

'Okay,' we said. 'Best of luck, Micky.'

Afterwards it occurred to me that Nash could have got in with one or other of us into a Hurricane and flown out – one pilot sitting on the other one's lap. It had been done before successfully. But none of us thought of it at the time.

We climbed back into our machines, all fingers and thumbs, reaching for the parachute straps which normally the groundstaff passed over your shoulders, shoving the ends into the quick-release button, scrabbling for the webbing harness, grabbing the helmet off the gunsight and jamming it on our heads, tubes dangling. There was a sense that at any moment yelling Japanese paratroopers would be pouring from the jungle. Out of the corner of my eye I saw Bertie's propeller start to turn, worryingly slowly, jerkily; but then there was a cough and it caught and fired to life. I pressed my own starter button and mine too, thank God, responded. Bertie and I thumbed up to each other and turned to wave goodbye to Micky Nash – but he had vanished into the jungle. The next time we were to see him was in Java, badly wounded by shrapnel from a hand grenade which had pierced his throat so that his voice seemed to issue from the hole in it rather than from his mouth. He had had a horrendous day, in which he had had to watch some of our own groundstaff being murdered by the paratroopers out of hand and see the wheels of a truck captured by the Japanese hovering over the edge of the ditch in which he had been hiding from them. It and all the other events of that truly dramatic day are fully recorded in my earlier books. Nash was to recover from his wounds – but it was only to be a respite. He was to escape with the rump of the squadron to Ceylon and do a tremendous amount of flying there and later in Burma – where, as General Slim was to record in his marvellous book *Defeat into Victory*, he was to be killed in a simple flying accident.

But all this was in the future so far as Bertie and I were concerned. A problem still remained – how to nurse two Hurricanes whose petrol gauges were reading all but empty over forty or so miles of impenetrable jungle to the safety of P.2. We both managed it, flying – as the expression went in those days – on sky hooks. Or, in other words, creeping at the slowest of speeds over the treetops. As we left P.1, knowing now what to look for, we could see what looked like white handkerchiefs caught in the branches of the forest, but were the parachutes of many Japanese. But that was all. The terrible jungle of Sumatra hid from our eyes all evidence of the drama taking place within it. And we had neither the time nor the capacity to dilly-dally – the tiny white patches on the green were come and gone in an instant, mere snapshots on the memory.

Recently there came back into my possession a book titled *Last Flight from Singapore* which was published by Macmillan in 1943. It was an account based on notes left by one of the five Americans in 258 Squadron, Arthur Gerald Donahue, of the experiences of its pilots in the Far East. A book which, so far as his personal action against the Japanese was concerned, basically came to a conclusion on the day following the paratroop attack.

When I returned to England after the war my parents gave me the copy they had guarded jealously because I had one or two mentions in it. At some stage, long before I started writing seriously, I must have lent it to a friend who failed to return it. Had I possessed a copy at the time I wrote *Hurricane Over the Jungle* and *Battle for Palembang* I would have certainly have quoted passages from it.

Donahue, who was to get what in the First World War was known as a 'Blighty One' (of which more later), was invalided home, and later that summer, while Acting Commanding Officer of an English squadron, failed to return from a flying mission. Amongst his effects was found the basic manuscript of *Last Flight from Singapore.*

The events of 14 February 1942 are to some extent chronicled in Donahue's book. I do not entirely agree with his version and there are, in fact, occasions where he was positively at fault. However, in all fairness and against the possibility that it is I who is in error, I quote (in part) Donahue's version of the latter part of the events.

Our C.O. who was leading the formation finally called it a day and led us back towards Palembang. As we neared the city we had to come down through a lot of cloud, and in doing so our formation got broken up so that when we came underneath, the two squadrons were separated.

I was leading a pair to the left and behind the C.O. Looking back I could see several machines a couple of miles behind, and one of them seemed to be diving towards another that was lower down. I was just a little suspicious, not enough to call out a warning, but keeping my eye on what was going on back there, until it was too late. Four long thin white lines suddenly reached out ahead from the plane that was diving, converging on the one in front of it – tracers – and then the one in front dived away leaving a thick trail of steam and glycol smoke!

Someone was calling 'Look out – bandits!' and someone else called 'Tally Ho!' Everything seemed to be in confusion back there, a melee of airplanes milling around, while we in fromt wheeled round and headed back towards them. My number two broke away to chase after something he saw. A few seconds later I looked back to see a Navy Zero diving down on me, his big stubby round nose and silver-coloured propellor-spinner identifying him as an enemy even at quite a distance. Another was following him. I opened my throttle and swung around hard to face him. I was facing him before he could get within firing range and I thought it was going to be a head-on show, both of us coming straight on at each other, shooting, seeing who would give way first before we collided; but he didn't seem to want that now that he'd lost the chance, for surprise. Before we were within firing range of each other, he zoomed up away. His partner behind did likewise. They had all the advantage of height and speed so there was nothing I could do about it, and I lost track of them.

There were several other airplanes milling around an area two or three miles across and I joined in, intercepting different ones that all turned out to be Hurricanes when I got close enough for identification. The Navy Zeros appeared to have all left, and the skirmish was over,

It was just then that Control began broadcasting a rather unusual order: 'Hello Tiger and Evitt aircraft! All Tiger and Evitt aircraft! Don't land at your base! Do not land at your base! Go and land at B Airdrome! Land at B Airdrome!'

B Airdrome was the jungle airdrome south-west of Palembang. I couldn't understand why we were being sent there, but presumed our own field was bombed and unserviceable. I headed down the railway from Palembang and soon reached B Airdrome and landed as ordered.

In disagreeing with Donahue's account of our return from that fruitless mission I do not in any way impugn his sincerity. Donahue was a very brave man who was deservedly awarded the Distinguished Flying Cross and who had volunteered to fly with the Royal Air Force long before America visualised being involved in the conflict and I was on the very next day to observe from close at hand his resolve and ability. Nor do I believe he was the kind of man who would falsify events or embroider them.

I am convinced that Donahue must have transposed the events of another occasion into this sortie and for these reasons:

Firstly, the names of all pilots of 258 Squadron who were killed or who force-landed in the jungle and survived are entered in my Log Book and all are dated before 14 February. We were to have other losses but these were later – in Java. But Donahue's account refers to an aircraft diving down leaving a thick trail of steam and glycol smoke – and a glycol leak defines it as a Hurricane because the Zeros were air-cooled through their radial engines while the Hurricane's coolant was glycol.

Secondly, when Thomson changed the heading from P.1 to P.2 the formation was in order and intact. I know this positively because my position in the formation was towards the rear of it. Thomson changed the heading because of the instructions received from 'Control' which Donahue refers to and which of course neither Lambert nor I heard. And it was because he changed the heading, and the formation remained in order and intact and changed direction with him that I (having no intercommunication because my radio was duff) was obliged, having spotted these Navy 0s, to do the unthinkable and break formation and try to warn him by sign language. In a word the formation changed direction because of the warning from 'Control'. Until the warning came we were blissfully heading back to P.1; there was no question of the formation wheeling round to face the enemy and then later receiving 'Control's' warning.

What I believe has happened is that Donahue has intermingled two separate incidents. These were hectic and dramatic days with incidents, including mêlées with Japanese fighters, occurring from day to day and sometimes from hour to hour. Donahue (who had written an earlier book: *Tally Ho! Yankee in a Spitfire*) would have been taking notes rather than writing a full-blown book at the time and it is from these notes that he would later have compiled the manuscript of *Last Flight from Singapore*. But this manuscript would not have been written at the time. With so much happening and so much movement from one place to another there simply would not have been the time or opportunity. Moreover, on the following day Donahue was to be wounded and hospitalised and it is very unlikely he would have even made notes of the events of 14 February at the time. It would certainly have been later, when he had been invalided away from the Dutch East Indies, that he would have turned any notes he had made into a manuscript. And then, split up from the other members of the squadron, he would not have had the opportunity of checking his memory against those of others, and would have done the best he could with the material at his disposal.

On the other hand I shared months of prisoner of war existence with several of the 258 Squadron pilots, with whom I would have discussed these events, if only because as a prisoner of war one has to fill in time somehow. And since the war I have met other 258 pilots who took part in these stirring days. Had my account of the return towards P.1 and diversion of most to P.2 been inaccurate, I am sure I would have been corrected.

CLOUD COVER

S o far as I know there was no roll call taken in the restaurant above the Luxor Cinema in Palembang on the night 14 February 1942 – and indeed there would have been no point in one being taken.

The fourteen pilots who had taken off from P.1 that morning were not necessarily all of 258 Squadron – in fact the likelihood is that some of them were of 232 Squadron. So it is quite possible that some of the 258 Squadron pilots may well have eaten in the restaurant that evening – those who were not on readiness at the time the paratroops were dropped on P.1, having most probably spent the day in town. But those who *had* been flying had all landed at P.2 and spent the remainder of the day and the following night there in some sort of building close by the airfield.

One would have thought that with so much to recount and so much to discuss, that afternoon, evening and night would have been indelibly imprinted on one's memory, but in fact, apart from a vague recollection that we spent a night of considerable discomfort ravaged by mosquitos and sleeping as best we could on the floor, or in chairs or on tables, it has quite passed from mine. I suppose that for all their discomfort those hours, being sandwiched as they were between two days of unsurpassable drama, seemed at the time of small account.

So the Hurricane pilots at P.2 – presumably limited to those who had taken part in the previous day's abortive mission – would have numbered amongst their members pilots of both 232 and 258 Squadrons but of the latter I can name for certain only Lambert, our Australian, Sheerin, our surviving Canadian, Scott, Donahue and myself. Whether or not Thomson was there I cannot say – it could well be that after landing there, for some reason he made his way to the town by road.

If I had to ascribe my salvation on 14 February to the actions of one man it would have been to Wilson at Montrose. Had it not been for his hare-brained low flying which pride obliged me to emulate, I would not have shaken off that Jap. Now, on the following day the actions of another man were to save my bacon.

That man was Art Donahue.

Arthur Gerald Donahue (known sometimes as 'Shorty' (for he was very small), brought up on his parents' farm in St Charles, Minnesota, learnt to fly in his state at Conrad Airport, Winona, and for a short period after the war broke out was instructing on an aerodrome near Laredo, Texas before joining the RAF in Canada in June 1940. He was one of the seven Americans who took part in the Battle of Britain and probably the first to have been in actual aerial combat. He was credited with the destruction of a Messerschmitt over the English Channel, with carrying out many reconnaissance sorties and success-fully attacking shipping and ground facilities. Shot down and badly burnt around ankles, wrists and face, he returned on leave to Minnesota in March, 1941. As quite possibly the only American in the States at the time who had actually seen action, he was eagerly inter-viewed at his home by the *Saturday Evening Post* and asked if he would be interested in sending them stories for publication. The idea didn't enthuse him and he suggested instead writing a book and the *Post* agreed to publish it no matter what. On the strength of this Donahue bought a typewriter, took it back with him to England and wrote *Tally Ho! Yankee in a Spitfire*. This was published simultaneously in the States and in England.

Having rejoined his Spitfire squadron, Donahue was busy doing reconnaissances and what were later to be called 'Intruder' operations over the Channel and northern France when he was invited by Squadron Leader Thomson, who had at one time been his Flight Commander, to join the farewell to England party for the pilots of 258 Squadron, to which Thomson had just been posted as Commanding Officer. Winter was settling in, bringing the threat of inactivity and months of bad weather, and Donahue was without much difficulty per-suaded by Thomson to throw in his lot with 258.

It was at Debden that 'Red' Campbell met him for the first time – and Campbell had heard a few stories, including the fact that Donahue had gone for a short time to the first Eagle Squadron then being put together, but had quickly rejoined his own Spitfire squadron because as he had remarked: 'It looked like the Eagle Squadron wasn't going to go to any place in a hurry when all they had was a bunch of Masters and Buffaloes!'

Campbell's first impression of Donahue had been an unfavourable one because he had a habit of standing by a bar with his hand hooked into his top button while he was drinking his beer, in other words, or rather in RAF slang, 'shooting a line'. But later, when they had become firm friends, Campbell discovered that one of the effects of Donahue's burns was pain when his hands were hanging, and supporting them in this way brought relief.

This, then, was the man who was to deliver me my seventh life as a fighter pilot.

As he writes in *Last Flight from Singapore*, he had been instructed on the previous evening by a telephone call from Thomson – who surely *must* have been elsewhere by now if he had to use a telephone – that he was to lead the six Hurricanes left in *our* Squadron on a dawn operation, and Donahue does refer to six Hurricanes taking part in the first morning sortie. In actual fact there were eight serviceable Hurricanes available on P.2 first thing that morning and it was arranged that they would be flown alternately by pilots of 258 and 232 Squadrons, with their missions to attack Japanese troops known to be making their way up the Moesi River towards Palembang in open invasion barges.

As one of those due to take part in the first sortie, I made my way out to my machine, and while doing so noticed that the sky was un-usually hazy, but neither I nor any of the others attached significance to this.

P.2 being a vast sprawling jungle airfield – by far the largest military airfield I have ever seen in my life – we took off in loose formation. Donahue, in his account of what was to follow, writes of turning at the end of the runway and not waiting for the rest of us to get into forma-tion with him. This is incorrect – P.2 had no runway and we did take off in a loose formation – if we had taken off singly the difficulties which were to arise for some of us would not have occurred.

That we had a problem became apparent even before we had our wheels up and locked into position, for the faint haze we had observed, through which from underneath it seemed one could see the blue sky, proved to be a wafer-thin layer of fog which, once we had passed through it, was discovered to be a sheet stretching as far as the eye could see in all directions, seeming to cover the whole of Sumatra!

So we broke through this cloud – if such a thin layer merited this description – and all of us were immediately aware that we were, as Donahue was to put it, 'in a terrible jam!' Even for those whose radios happened to be functioning properly there was no way of getting talked down again onto P.2. And a Hurricane moves swiftly, and by the time we had locked away our undercarriages and come to terms with the situation, we had left the field far behind. To land back on it we would need to do a circuit and then trust to luck that after descending through that thin (but from above opaque) sheet, we would find ourselves over the airfield itself and not about to smash into the jungle's roof. And even though P.2 was of such an enormous length the chances of making a blind approach sufficiently correct once having quit the field were absolutely minimal – and with every second while we considered our alternatives, becoming more and more so.

So what *were* these alternatives? Well, even if P.1 was by some miracle not covered by the mist, it was almost certainly by now occupied by the Japanese paratroops, and having once landed amongst them and got away with it, I for one didn't consider that much of an option. And if there were any other airfields in Sumatra we didn't know where they were, and anyway, by the look of the brilliant white cloud sheet glistening below us in the early morning sun, the probability was that they'd be under the mantle too.

There was, of course, Java. For the life of me now I can't remember whether our Hurricanes were still fitted with long-range tanks when we flew from Kemajoran in Java to P.2 in Sumatra. I rather think they may have been, for I see from my Log Book that the flights from Java to Sumatra, and then from Sumatra to Singapore were of two and a quarter hours' and two and a half hours' duration respectively, and they could only have taken as long as that if we had been flying at the slow speed instructed when long-range tanks were fitted. So at the time I was not absolutely certain that without long-range tanks we had the range to make Java although I believed it should be possible to get there reasonably comfortably providing the decision was taken without too much delay. But there was obviously no future in messing around overlong if Java was to be the final destination.

An alternative ploy was (like an airliner stacked up over Heathrow) to tool around the sky in some sort of holding pattern in the hope that by the time the mist cleared one would still have enough petrol to relocate P.2 and get down on it.

Or, *in extremis,* one *could* bale out, although the prospect of descending through a layer of mist into a fetid jungle swarming with wild animals, crocodiles, snakes, bugs and Lord knows what else – or of ending up dangling fifty or a hundred feet above the ground from the branches of some huge tree – was hardly appealing.

I suppose we all must have wasted about five minutes (during which we orbited over where we hoped P.2 approximately lay) to consider these alternatives. Of them I preferred the head-for-Java option. The jungle, I remembered, was rather less dense the nearer one got to Java, and if the mist didn't clear and my petrol was obviously going to run out, then my chances if I had to bale out or attempt a forced landing would be marginally better the further south I was.

On the other hand if we quit Sumatra this would bring about the removal of almost the entire fighter strike force capable of attacking the river-borne Japanese invaders.

While such thoughts were no doubt occupying all of our minds, vital seconds were ticking by and P.2 had vanished. It was down there somewhere; but somewhere is not good enough when what has to be done is to descend through cloud whose base is barely above, if indeed it was above, tree-top height – for in his book Donahue refers to wisps of fog amongst the treetops. Even with flaps lowered the stalling speed of a Hurricane – and therefore the slowest approach for landing speed – was, so far as I remember, about sixty miles an hour, which is eighty-eight feet per second. And at eighty-eight feet per second there isn't much margin for recovery if, as you break cloud, you see a tree directly ahead of you!

Fortunately, and most unexpectedly, help was at hand. Of a sudden a green ball of light followed by a trail of white smoke burst through the cloud sheet. The sense of relief was overwhelming for it was immediately obvious what was happening. Someone down there, listening horror-stricken to the sound of our Merlin engines, had with energy and imagination got hold of a Very pistol and some cartridges and was firing them to indicate where P.2 lay.

That someone was, in fact, Arthur Donahue. As he entered the mist on take-off, alert enough to realise the danger, he had at once banged down his undercarriage lever and, with the sprawling airfield easily long enough, was able to land on his take-off run. Taxying his Hurricane as fast as he dared over the bumpy ground he got to the operational area, leapt from his Hurricane, demanded and obtained a Very pistol and a supply of cartridges, and racing out towards the middle of the field started firing cartridges through the mist at intervals.

If our problems were not entirely solved at least the alternative of abandoning Sumatra and heading for Java no longer applied. So long as the supply of cartridges held out we knew with reasonable accuracy where P.2 was. What, of course, we didn't know was where on P.2 whoever was firing the cartridges was standing. He could be at one side or the other or at the centre; at one end or the other or in the middle. Nor could we judge from a single coloured ball with any accuracy which way the unseen airfield beneath us was orientated. So far as this aspect of the business was concerned we could only make a fair appraisal by noting the angle of the sun and recalling, somewhat uncertainly, the general orientation of P.2.

But – and this was the important thing – we had a guide.

The first thing we had to do was to lower our wheels and flaps preparatory to attempting a landing, and to this day I remember the remarkable sight of half a dozen Hurricanes, with wheels and flaps down, gyrating round an occasional Roman Candle. It was a sight never before seen or imagined, at once unreal and comical.

And it soon became stranger still.

One pilot, like an enthusiastic swimmer on a winter's day, decided to take the plunge, dropped the nose of his Hurricane and disappeared momentarily into the mist only to rear up again almost at once in an evasive climb, having obviously barely avoided colliding with the trees. And back he came to rejoin us and creep round the circle, his wheels turning slowly – and that, I think, was the most mesmerising thing of all – those slow-turning wheels!

After a minute or so, another pilot took the plunge – what happened to him we, the remainder, had no idea. He didn't reappear – perhaps he was taxying gratefully in to receive the congratulations of the watchers and listeners down below – or perhaps he was dead.

Although it is clear from *Last Flight from Singapore* Donahue believed he was the only pilot who acted quickly enough to avoid getting stuck up above the mist, in fact Lambert had been equally alert. So now from six, we were down to five – or to be more accurate, down to five Hurricanes and one Blenheim. Where that Blenheim came from I have no idea. I suppose he was up there waiting to guide us to our targets. And what happened to that Blenheim, I have no idea either. For a while he kept us company, then he was gone. With his longer range the problem would have been a less pressing one for the pilot and being, with wheels and flaps down, much more cumbersome than a Hurricane, it was hardly the type of aircraft in which to attempt what we were obliged to. Most probably he hied off to Java leaving a now-diminished circle of Hurricanes creeping round with their slowly spinning wheels and, some of the time, with lowered flaps as well.

I took my turn in an attempted descent, gingerly descending into the wool. For an instant only all was white and then, suddenly, it was jungle green and I was slamming the throttle open and rearing up like a startled hare into the clear air above.

Again I tried, and this time found the airfield but, instead of travelling along its length I was crossing it diagonally. And so on. I tried several times and couldn't manage to get it right enough although once or twice I did get very near. Each time I was either overshooting or too much to one side, or in one case, heading directly for the clump of trees which, remarkably, grew in the airfield's centre.

Meanwhile, depressingly, the circle was diminishing in number and two questions were hammering in my brain. The first, if I abandoned what was beginning to look suspiciously like an attempt to kill myself, would I by now have enough petrol to get me to Kemajoran anyway? And the second, how many Very flares did they have down there? There couldn't be all that large a stock and once they ran out, then that would be the end of it.

There was a curious similarity between my Montrose experiences of losing myself in cloud, losing myself at night and smashing through those fir trees with Willis. But so far as the first two of these was concerned, one thing was sure: if I had known that Montrose airfield was down below nothing would have driven me away from it.

I realised that if I was to survive, I had to think intelligently; had to abandon this hit-and-miss business and work out some sort of plan. The first thing, obviously, was to find out and store in my mind the directional bearing of the central axis of this strange-shaped jungle airfield. And that, I told myself, shouldn't be too difficult, particularly if I made a feint with wheels and flaps up which would give me far greater control of my machine.

So that was what I did and it told me what I wanted, and now the problem was at least reduced to one of length and width. How to solve it? The field was very long but in part relatively narrow because it was waisted in the middle, and the trees growing there added to the difficulty. But at either end it was considerably wider so that looked at from above it had a double keyhole shape. This offered a solution.

Uneasily aware that by now there were only a couple more Hurricanes as well as myself still trying to get down, I waited for the next rising ball and when it came headed directly to it. Using the residual smoke as a marker point I flew at right angles to what I had calculated was the longitudinal axis of the airfield and started counting. I then made a right-angle turn and counted off the same number, and then a third right-angle, again counting. If I had it correctly when I turned my fourth right-angle, I ought to be heading more or less in the right direction for an approach and I ought to have some rough idea how far away P.2 was. What, of course, I wouldn't know was where exactly on the airfield whoever was firing the Very pistol was standing but that was a chance I would have to take.

Another Roman Candle at this juncture would have been very nice but I didn't get it. So I set my course, counted off half my number, lowered wheels and flaps and entered the mist.

When I broke through I was a trifle too much to the right and there were trees below me and I was too far along the airfield's length – but nothing was going to have me go up through that lot again. I sideslipped off height to the left, clearing me from the trees and putting me over the landing field itself. But I was too far along by now to avoid running into the jungle at the end but with, I believed, just sufficient room for manoeuvre. When the field began to open out at the northern keyhole end, I put on a little right bank to follow its perimeter and then when as near to the trees as I dared risk go, slammed the throttle fully open and brought the stick hard over to the left and back, putting the Hurricane into a steep left-hand turn. I was very low, a matter of fifty feet or so. I had wheels and flaps down and, of course, once into the turn couldn't see the trees I was obviously going to hit if my turn wasn't steep enough; on the other hand I did have a clear vision of the airfield in the direction in which I hoped to land. The knot of trees in its middle was an added problem but the really important thing exercising my mind was how steep I dared make my turn without causing an incipient spin. I am satisfied in my mind that but for the practice, *force majeure*, I had had with Wilson in Montrose I would not have judged it correctly. As it was, I did. I got round the turn, took off the bank, got straight, banked a bit again to avoid the knot of trees and straightened up again, I was going very fast but fortunately P.2 had the length I needed – I fishtailed furiously and made it.

My Log Book tells me the whole exercise took forty minutes. As I taxied in I saw two of our precious Hurricanes on their noses.

Donahue dealt with my landing rather more briefly than I have:

> One of the Hurricanes managed to break into sight more or less directly over the edge of the field and by means of a hair-raising vertical turn close to the ground in order to get in line with the runway, and some violent fish-tailing to kill his speed, the pilot made it. He came taxying back, and I saw it was Kelly. He grinned at me and made a motion of wiping sweat from his forehead. I held up clasped hands in congratulation.

It had been a very dramatic start to what was to prove a very full and exciting day but bearing in mind the title of this book I must resist doing any more than giving a brief précis of the balance.

When the mist cleared 232 and 258 Squadrons took it in turns to attack the Japanese motoring upstream of the River Moesi to invest Palembang. It was on one of these attacks that Donahue got his Blighty One.

We attacked in pairs and I was flying as Number Two to Donahue and, being in line astern behind him, had an excellent view of his last flying sortie in the Far East.

The Japanese were jammed into these long oblong self-propelled barges like matches in a box and, the river being straight at the place where we came upon them, were stretched in a long line close to the northern bank, presumably to obtain as much cover as the currents and shallows allowed. I did not make a note of how many there were of them but I suppose there were perhaps half a dozen with imaginably about two hundred men in each. Their sole defence was a machine-gunner mounted at the stern of each, for the soldiers were so jammed against each other that they could hardly have raised their arms to fire at us.

With our Hurricanes having a fire-power of about 12,000 rounds a minute and the guns being loaded with, in addition to normal ammunition, a leavening of tracer, incendiary and armour-piercing bullets, as was normal in air warfare, the slaughter we inflicted was fearsome.

Donahue's attack was superbly done. Having spotted the barges, we orbited to come on them from behind in a direct line, and as I had throttled back to avoid any risk of hitting Donahue when I pulled out from my first attack, I had the clearest picture of it. I do not believe he missed a barge, his guns raking each from stern to stem and making a pincushion of the water between each of them. The flicker of the defending gunners was like torches being switched on and off, and this was echoed by the pinpoints of light of Donahue's bullets finding their targets amongst the helpless Japanese.

Following behind Donahue I made my own first attack, and to my surprise, when I pulled out to orbit to make another, I lost sight of him. I learnt the reason later – he had been hit by bullets from one of the machine-gunners and was wounded badly in one leg. With great difficulty he made his way back to P.2, where he made a successful if somewhat clumsy landing. Lifted out of his machine, he had a field dressing applied to his wound and was then evacuated to Java in a Lockheed Hudson. After a few days in hospital in Bandoeng he boarded a ship in Batavia. By August he was back in England and by now, fully recovered from his wound, was soon flying again. But sadly not for long. As written earlier he went missing over the English Channel and his body was never found. His death is recorded officially as taking place on 11 September 1942.

The fuller details of our attacks on the invasion barges are recorded in Donahue's *Last Flight from Singapore* and, for that matter, in my own earlier books.

For my own part, having completed my own attacks, I returned to P.2 and, having made two more flights that day and the decision having been taken to evacuate P.2 (one wonders why, with the

Japanese still forty miles distant from it and quite unaware of its existence), I was fortunate enough to be able to find a Hurricane in which to fly down to Batavia.

There is a curious postscript to this event. With more pilots than Hurricanes for them to fly, some of us were told to get down to Java as best we could. Four of us, Lambert, Scott, Miller and myself, headed along a track which ended at a T-junction. After a council of war Lambert and I decided to make for the airfield, hoping we might somehow get a lift down to Kemajoran. The other two headed for the railway station and, having got down by train to the southernmost port of Sumatra, boarded a ship bound for Java. When it arrived at the port of Tandjeonpriok, its captain, who saw no sense in depositing two by now very experienced pilots on an island which he foresaw would shortly fall to the Japanese, refused to allow them ashore and, when he sailed for Colombo, took them with him. Miller, after years of flying in Burma, was to survive the war, but Scott was to be killed accidentally when the pilot of another Hurricane with whom he was practising dog-fighting pressed the button of his machine guns instead of his gun camera and shot him down.

Astonishingly, Lambert and I found two Hurricanes still available on P.2. I cannot vouch for Lambert's, but so far as mine was concerned the groundstaff warned me against trying to take it off as there was something radically wrong with it. I decided to ignore their warning. There certainly was something wrong with it somewhere, because as I opened the throttle it veered frighteningly to the left and I missed hitting a large black shed by what felt like inches. But I don't recall any problem in the flight down to Java, nor on landing.

Many years later a man who had been a prisoner of war with me, and for nearly three years in Japan had shared the same table at which we ate, telephoned me to tell me about a painting with the title 'Departure from P.2' that was for sale at an aeronautical artists' exhibition in Derby which he thought would interest me. My wife and I went to have a look at it and discovered it to be a painting by Miles O'Reilly of a single Hurricane taking off from a jungle airfield. Having bought the painting I contacted O'Reilly to discover that it had been inspired by my account in *Hurricane Over the Jungle* of taking off that last, and theoretically unserviceable Hurricane, from P.2. A reproduction of O'Reilly's painting was used by the publishers of my *Battle for Palembang* for the jacket cover.

THROUGH THE SOUND BARRIER

S INGAPORE having fallen, and orders having been given for the complete withdrawal from Sumatra, with the Dutch (with the honourable exception of their Navy) showing no intention of putting up any sort of resistance to the Japanese in Java, the Allies ought to have concentrated on getting as many personnel away to Colombo or Australia as was still possible in the days remaining before the invasion of Java, which was obviously imminent. And this, I suggest, in particular applied to evacuating the surviving pilots who, after several weeks of concentrated battle experience, had matured from being, frankly, amateurs into seasoned professionals.

Until now the losses in fighter pilots had been very heavy. There had been two New Zealand Squadrons originally in Singapore, one was 453 and the other 488. Equipped with Brewster Buffaloes, they had been no match for the Japanese in their Zeros, and they had been decimated, with only a few survivors available to fly Hurricanes when at last some were available to them.

The first Hurricanes in Singapore were flown by 232 Squadron (whose original pilots consisted of six each of a group of four separate squadrons: 17, 135, 136 and 232), which was *en route* to the Middle East. Only six pilots of each of these four squadrons were with the convoy, the balance of seventy-two pilots being due to follow by a different route. When the Japanese declared war, a part of the convoy including these twenty-four pilots, together with fifty-one Hurricanes, was detached at Durban on 24 December and diverted to Singapore. It arrived in the harbour on 13 January and was only saved from destruction in a most determined bombing attack when a fierce tropical storm blew up.

Meanwhile the balance of 232 Squadron's pilots (in fact nineteen in number) had sailed on a troopship, and having arrived at Freetown on 23 December, sailed on to Takoradi, where they disembarked on 29 December and then flew across Africa to Wadi Saidna, near Khartoum, in a Pan American aircraft, as had 258 Squadron. This

The last air pictures of Singapore. Taken by Donahue from his Hurricane when leaving the island for Sumatra.

second complement of 232 Squadron made up its number to the standard twenty-four *en route* by the inclusion of pilots from 605 Squadron, who, like those of 258 Squadron, had been stranded at Gibraltar with the sinking of *Ark Royal.* These twenty-four 232 Squadron pilots also flew off *Indomitable* to Java, twenty-three arriving.

Thus, theoretically, 232 Squadron had forty-eight pilots: the original twenty-four from the Durban to Singapore convoy, and the twenty-four off *Indomitable.* But in fact it was never fully integrated as a complete unit, and quite a number of the second batch of twenty-four never got farther than Java.

Meanwhile the losses of the first twenty-four to arrive in Singapore were truly horrendous. At least thirteen had been either killed or badly wounded within the first week of flying. By the time the second batch flew off *Indomitable* 232 Squadron had suffered three further losses and by the time Sumatra was evacuated only twenty-three of the original forty-eight survived, with some of these wounded and others, for one reason or another, almost without battle experience.

Meanwhile the number of my own squadron, 258, had through death and injury been reduced from twenty-four to fifteen. At this point it was decided by the higher authorities that of these fifteen, six should stay behind (together with six made up out of surviving 488, 232 and 605 Squadron pilots) and become members of 605 Squadron, most of whose groundstaff, having served magnificently in Sumatra, had somehow or other made their way back to Java. Thus a dozen or so pilots were to stay on to fly the last few Hurricanes which remained while the rest were to be evacuated to Colombo.

The fateful morning dawned when the decision as to which of 258's pilots should stay on was to be made. All surviving pilots of the squadron assembled at the Hotel des Indes in Batavia together with one or two other pilots who happened to be present in the hotel. Thomson gave out the news and, having required one of the New Zealanders, Harry Dobbyn, to remain as a Flight Commander, called for volunteers to stay with him. 'Red' Campbell obliged. Cards were then cut for the other four – the low cards being drawn by Nichols, Healey, Lambert and myself. However, Nichols having recently crash-landed after being in action in Sumatra, another New Zealander, John Vibert, volunteered to take his place.

With the Japanese now turning their attention to Java, this meagre force of fighters operating from the military airfield of Tjillillitan, now the civilian airport of Perdanakusama, soon suffered losses. Of those who had been of 258 Squadron, Dobbyn was shot down and killed and Campbell was not to fly again, having also been shot down and only

Author and Lambert at readiness at Tjillillitan airfield, Java.

managing to bale out by butting his way out of a cockpit whose hood had jammed shut, injuring himself in the process.

Thus of the original twenty-four 258 Squadron pilots only three (Healey, Lambert and myself) assisted by the volunteer, John Vibert, went on flying in the Far East to the bitter end.

As can be imagined these last few days were very busy ones, with the Japanese paying particular attention to the airfield from which we were operating, and our survival in spite of always being outnumbered many times by flocks of Navy 0s escorting the daily flights of bombers can only be ascribed to the hard-won experience gained through the past few weeks.

But, using tactics which we had discussed in depth and agreed upon, survive we did without further losses, although I suppose there wasn't one of us who wouldn't have admitted he was lucky to do so.

However, in selecting my eighth life, I am not going to choose an aerial battle with a Navy 0. As I have written before that sort of thing is after all part and parcel of what a fighter pilot must expect and if you picked on every such encounter you'd soon be way beyond the definitive nine.

*　　*　　*

The tactics for survival which we hammered out between the four of us were very simple and were based on what we had discovered by now were the positive advantages the Hurricane enjoyed over its rival, the Navy 0. We had learnt to our cost where the Japanese would have the advantage: they would vastly outnumber us and they could out-turn us. So getting involved in dogfighting was no more than a short cut to suicide. On the other hand we could fly to heights which the Japanese fighters simply could not reach, we had the better fire-power and we could subject our Hurricanes to stresses which Navy 0s could not tolerate.

As distinct from the situation on P.1, here on Tjillillitan we normally had reasonably good warning of the approach of the Japanese air armadas as these had been spotted and notified to Java by watchers on some of the myriad of small islands over which they had to pass *en route*. So, we reasoned, the intelligent thing for us to do on 'scramble!' was to get up to 30,000 feet or so as quickly as we could and wait for the enemy fighters and bombers to appear below us and then, at our leisure, pick on a target, have a shot at it and then with no more ado break off and dive, calculating that no Navy 0 could follow us far down without the gravest risk that it would dis-integrate when pulling out of a power dive which a Hurricane could cope with without difficulty.

We did not claim amongst ourselves, nor do I do so now, that such were the bravest of all tactics. They were not. They were tactics for survival with the spin-off that so long as there were always Hurricanes, however few, waiting to attack the bombers, the Japanese would need to escort them with fighters of their own which could have been employed usefully elsewhere.

My eighth life came about on one of these occasions. I do not have the date as the entries in my Log Book covering the Java period simply lists 'scrambles!' with a few side notes; but it would be somewhere between 24 and 28 February 1942.

Having reached our altitude, we observed Navy 0s orbiting below us in a chasm between two towering blocks of cumulus cloud and, seeing no bombers, elected to have a shot at them. Being impatient by nature, and only for that reason, I was the first to have a go, and having made my attack, with a throttle opened wide, hauled over into a vertical dive.

As I was going down I looked over my shoulder and saw one of the most remarkable, and in its way most beautiful sights I have ever seen. As I have written there was a chasm between two enormous towers of cumulus cloud and clearly etched against the backdrop of one of these

I could see the other three Hurricanes diving down and, peeling off to follow them, the whole formation of Navy 0s.

I do not believe any film director could have filmed a more dramatic sight, and I was so utterly mesmerised looking at it that for the moment I forgot everything else. Every aircraft was sharp and clear against the backdrop of gleaming white cumulus. It was a film set, gigantic in scale with the actors miniscule but giving it life – twenty or more aircraft all in a screaming power dive. It was totally unforgettable.

I watched for far too long. By the time I looked away I must have dived straight down with a fully opened throttle some seven or eight thousand feet and when I tried to start easing out, I found my controls were locked.

Slamming the throttle shut and putting both hands on the control column, I hauled on it with all my strength, thrusting with my feet against the rudder bar to obtain maximum purchase, but it was to absolutely no effect. I was travelling too fast and my controls were frozen solid. I do not remember that I was afraid and I do not believe I was. There was too little time to be afraid and too much to do.

In the old days, and maybe now when films are made showing pilots in similar situations a little extra drama is added to the situation by such devices as showing blood leaking from the pilot's nostrils or from the corners of his mouth, or having him yell or scream in anguish. In fact nothing so nonsensical occurs – you just understand very clearly the predicament you are in and that if you don't find a way of getting out of it, you will very soon be dead. Nor does the whole of your past life flash before you; nor even do you have visions of that dreadful moment of final impact. You are far too busy.

It was obvious that baling out was not an alternative to be considered. At the sort of terminal velocity I had by now achieved, it struck me that if I did manage to get my head out of the cockpit as like as not it would be torn off by the slipstream and if it wasn't, then the tail fin of the Hurricane was ready and waiting to slice me in two. So that wasn't on.

That left just one other alternative. The tail trim.

In a Hurricane, as in other fighter aircraft, there were minute strips of metal like tiny elevators fitted to the trailing edges of the elevators which were adjustable by turning a relatively large wheel inside the cockpit. Like the smallest weights on a balance, these strips could be moved fractionally to give perfect fore and aft balance so that in normal flight the stick is absolutely neutral; indeed that is their purpose. One was always instructed to treat tail fins with great respect and it was said that misuse at high speeds could tear off the tailplane. Now to use these trims was Hobson's choice.

Taking one hand off the stick, I wound the trim wheel back towards myself and at once transferring this hand back to join its fellow, hauled back on the control column with all my strength. And I was rewarded by the faintest softness, the slightest yielding. Hanging on like grim death with one hand, thrusting with my feet, my back pressed hard against the shield of armour plate behind me, I clung to my gain and wound back the trim the merest fraction more and again grabbed at the stick and heaved. And I knew I was going to be all right – that I had left the vertical. I still had to be very careful – too much exuberance would pull the Hurricane apart. But I was winning. The G in my head was intense and the aircraft, normally so light and responsive, felt like a lorry load of lead and I could almost feel the huge strain on the wings myself. But I was winning. I began to see the red and green world – for red and green are the colours of Java, red soil, green growth – which had been fixed straight down ahead of me, start sliding away behind me as the nose came up, all the time accelerating until at length, there was the horizon in its proper place and I was flying straight and level!

I reversed the trim, busy talking to myself as I always did under this kind of circumstance. I looked at the altimeter and found it registering 15,000 feet. That was quite some dive, I told myself. I glanced at the airspeed indicator – and I couldn't believe my eyes. Only 300 miles an hour! Impossible! And it crossed my mind that if that was all that I was doing I'd soon have a shower of Navy 0s on my tail. Anyway, how could I be only doing 300 miles an hour after what had to have been a dive of terminal velocity? Then, glaring at the airspeed indicator, I saw that the speed was dropping fast – as it should be, I told myself, throttled right back as I was. And it was then the penny dropped. I'd gone right round the clock not once, but twice! Absolutely fascinated, I watched the instrument, saw it complete a counter revolution, pass through the 400 miles per hour figure at one o'clock on the inner scale and then through 240 miles an hour at five o'clock on the outer one. It should, I thought, be all right now. I pushed the throttle open experimentally and, after a moment or two, my speed began to pick up again.

There is a rule of thumb for converting true flying speed from the speed indicated by the instruments, which, working on pressure, underwrite your speed the higher you climb. For every thousand feet you add one and three-quarter per cent to the indicated speed. Even by the time I had pulled out to straight and level I had to have been flying at more than 590 miles an hour, and in the vertical I was certainly knocking the speed of sound if, in fact, I hadn't been through it.

I do not know if any other Hurricane pilot has actually claimed to have flown through the sound barrier. I am not now claiming to have done so myself. But I put it forward as a possibility for I have so much respect for the sturdiness of that wonderful aircraft, the Hurricane, to believe it could well be able to take the strain.

If it is to Arthur Donahue I owe my seventh life it is to the designer of the Hurricane, Sydney Camm, I owe my eighth. It is a truly remarkable achievement for the designer of an aircraft with a top straight and level speed of only 330 miles an hour that it could be put through such a test and emerge triumphant; it seemed at the time even more remarkable when compared with the disintegration of its rival in Palembang: the Navy 0, or Zero!

THREE DAY MARGIN

T HE balance of my wartime's flying can soon be told. We flew busily at Tjillillitan until 1 March 1942, when the Japanese invaded – one of their striking points being at Cheribon on the north coast of Java and well within our range.

My Log Book for that day records three scrambles. In the course of one of these, the four of us and an ex-605 Squadron pilot, *en route* to the invasion point, were diverted by a Japanese seaplane which was the very devil to shoot down, as it seemed to be able to turn on a sixpence. After the attack on it, which I was advised later was successful, four of the Hurricanes returned to Tjillillitan, presumably to re-arm. For my own part, I had the pleasure, when I made my first attack on it, of seeing it release the bombs or depth-charges it was carrying, which exploded in the sea below, causing a fascinating coral atoll pattern in the water, but what I could not see was the seaplane. This was because I found I had a dirty windscreen and whenever I got behind the seaplane to get a shot at it, it disappeared from sight, being of a curious greyish colour, which seemed to merge with the thin layer of oil, or whatever it was that was obscuring my vision. Moreoever, with four other Hurricanes, each eager to secure a victory and arriving from every quarter, it seemed to me that I was more at risk of colliding with one or other of them than shooting down the will-o'-the-wisp.

So I left the others to it and set off for the invasion point, where I strafed some Japanese coming ashore in various craft, shot up a bunch of Japanese setting up what looked like an anti-aircraft post and, coming on another seaplane drawn up in a tiny cove, was lucky enough to set it on fire. Hotly pursued by the shells of the escorting warships, I beetled back to Tjillillitan, where, shortly afterwards, we were told to hand over our few Hurricanes to the mixed bunch of 488 Squadron et cetera operating with us and make our escape from Java.

Had the Dutch been helpful, perhaps even at this late stage we might have got away and rejoined the balance of the squadron, which was to operate for the remainder of the war from Ceylon, and then from Burma, with (apart from the unfortunate accidents to Nash and Scott, and one pilot shot down and killed in the Japanese Easter Day raid on Colombo) only minor losses. However, for three precious days we were obliged to hang about purposelessly in Bandoeng, and by the time the Dutch agreed that we could go, in spite of that exciting, madcap drive on a wonderful moonlit night through Java to the southern port of Tjilatjap, by the time we got to the coast the last ship had sailed.

Having for 126 years years ruled the beautiful, mountainous island of Java some six hundred miles long and supporting at the time over sixty million souls, the Dutch high command yielded with hardly even token resistance to a negligible and poorly equipped Japanese invasion force, the capitulation taking place on 8 March 1942, by which time few of the fourteen thousand Allied servicemen (to say nothing of the Dutch) had fired a shot in anger, or indeed, been anywhere near the enemy!

For the next two weeks or so the roads of Java, winding their way through breathtakingly lovely hills and valleys, were clogged with convoys of soldiers and air force groundstaff, vaguely wandering around the country and wondering where to head for next. Rumour was rife and the only certain knowledge was that, so far as they were concerned, hostilities were over and escape by sea impossible because all ships which hadn't left in time had been sunk. But where the Japanese were was a mystery.

Eventually, coalescing into larger bodies, the Allied troops settled into large groups which descended on towns or on tea plantations with some sort of military command established but with, as yet, no sight of a single Japanese, and for a couple of weeks enjoyed a delightful and totally unreal Shangri-La existence. This was brutally brought to an end when the Japanese at last took control and dispatched arbitrarily selected groups to various prison or concentration camps.

The one in which I and the other surviving pilots of 258 Squadron found ourselves was the native gaol of Boei Glodok in Batavia – now demolished and its site occupied by a supermarket! Here I was to spend the next seven months whose unpleasantness was at least relieved by having the companionship of the pilots with whom I had shared the stirring days in Singapore, Palembang and Tjillillitan.

However, on 31 October I was parted from them, to board with a large clutch of other prisoners of war a ship sailing for Singapore and thence, after changing to another ship, to Japan itself.

The ship on which some twelve hundred prisoners of war and some one thousand Japanese soldiers were accommodated was the old, rusting, dilapidated *Dai Nichi Maru* (which, roughly translated, means

Great Day!), built before the turn of the century and weighing about four thousand tons.

It has generally been accepted that the voyage of the *Dai Nichi Maru* from Singapore to Moji in Japan was one of the most horrendous of the many vile voyages which Japanese prisoners of war were forced to endure. As I have dealt with it in detail in my book *Living With Japanese* and have used it as the basis of one of my novels *Fepow – The Story of a Voyage Beyond Belief,* I will merely sketch in a few facts to convey some idea of its awfulness.

The hold in which I spent those terrible weeks measured 60 feet by 80 feet and was two decks down; it had an open hatch about 20 feet square roughly central to it. The floor was a consignment of wet iron ore which had been levelled immediately below the hatch opening and then sloped down at an angle of about thirty degrees in all directions until it met either the ribs of the ship or the bulkhead of the adjoining hold. Lighting was by means of a single electric light bulb hanging on a flex in the hatch opening which cast illumination little farther than the levelled patch, beyond which gloom merged into Stygian blackness. The hold was alive with rats, flies and cockroaches; access was by means of a single vertical iron ladder; furnishings consisted of a few dozen planks and straw mats. This was to be the home for 268 men in moderate health, dressed for the tropics, for a journey of thirty days into the Japanese winter.

It was not long before sickness struck, this taking the form of diarrhoea and before long there were few who were not afflicted. To pass a motion a man had to climb the iron ladder to use one of the few rough wooden lavatories built out over the side of the ship, and before long there were many men unable to achieve this, so that the hold soon became utterly contaminated with blood and mucus.

With each passing day the weather deteriorated. From time to time heavy rain poured down into the hold, and as the temperature fell, on some occasions even snow. Inordinately rough seas added to the general discomfort, and the food, for those still with the stomach, or even the capacity to eat it, was appalling.

About one third of the men who boarded the *Dai Nichi Maru* in Keppel Harbour, Singapore, were to die either on board or in their prison camp as a direct result of that dreadful voyage and those who died, died in fearful agony and without dignity. After a showpiece funeral by the Japanese for the first man to die, the bodies of those who followed were simply pitched overboard.

At Moji the survivors were arbitrarily divided into small groups for transit to different prison camps, the one in which I found myself

Innoshima Prisoner of War Camp-Japan

Geoffrey S. Coxhead

Nov 27· 1942 to SEP 15 1945.

containing originally one hundred and ending up on the small island of Innoshima in the Inland Sea of Japan.

The camp (in order to give the appearance of complying with Red Cross requirements that prisoners of war should from time to time be moved to a different camp) bore the various titles of Fukuoka 12, Zentsuji 2 and finally Hiroshima 5. Although we hardly thought so at the time, in comparison with others it wasn't too bad a camp. We had our illnesses, deaths, beatings, over-work and near-starvation at the end, but the surroundings were very beautiful and the Hitachi Dockyard in which we were to toil for nearly three years was preferable to coal or copper mines, or creating railways or airfields in tropical jungles.

The make-up of our complement was interesting and, I think, unique. We were, for a prison camp, comparatively few in number – if none had died or left the camp to be sent elsewhere our complement would have been two hundred. Half of the inmates were ex-colonials from Hong Kong, mainly civilians who as members of the Hong Kong Volunteer Defence Corps became soldiers for a few days of their life. These were men who had been bankers, judges, lawyers, shipowners, taipans, who knew the Orient and those who lived in it, whose education, background and clout put them poles apart from the largely raw,

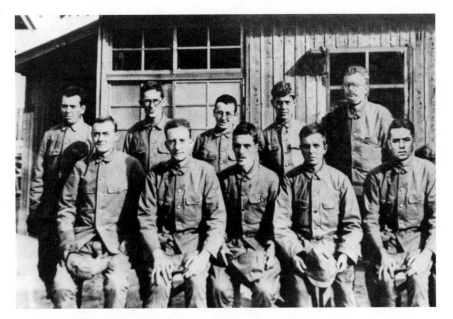

Prisoners in Japan including author, front row, left.

unfledged RAF groundstaff beside whom they were going to have to work as dockyard coolies. It was an extraordinary mixture. A man with the ambition to arrange the social experiment of forcing two groups of men utterly disparate in age, class and experience to live and work together could hardly have chosen a better setting.

I have included the above few paragraphs to give a snapshot against which the event which I have chosen as my ninth life as a fighter pilot can be viewed. Any reader who is interested in a broader picture can obtain it by reading my *Living With Japanese* which covers those years in detail.

The event which gave the final wartime life not only to me personally but probably to every single prisoner of war of the Japanese was the dropping of the atom bomb on Hiroshima. But whereas in other camps the connection, although valid enough, was to a degree an indirect one, in our case it was very positive.

Through the last months of the Pacific War the Allies had total control of the skies. The first hint to us that this was so occurred on 19 March 1942 when our dockyard was attacked by fighter-bombers flown off aircraft carriers. The damage inflicted was only light but the morale boost was tremendous.

A damaged and sunken freighter moored by the quayside.

Through the weeks that followed, many solitary American B-29 bombers and other individual aircraft, clearly on reconnaissance missions, flew over or in the neighbourhood of the dockyard, maintaining a steady course and a fair altitude, all unmolested by either Japanese fighters or ground defence. On only one occasion did we see both an American and a Japanese aircraft in the sky at the same time, and the latter, a seaplane, promptly fled.

However, from about 9 May things took a more portentous turn. It was a glorious day, with winter turning into spring and the sky about one-fifth covered by cumulus cloud. At about 10.00 a.m. the air raid warning – the *keikaikeiho* – was sounded in the dockyard and very soon the drone of approaching aircraft could be heard. The drone grew steadily but still no aircraft came in sight and it was not until the sky was vibrant with the roar of approaching bombers that the first group of B-24s or B-29s emerged, in perfect V-formation at (at a guess) about fifteen thousand feet, from a towering bank of cumulus just a little to the south of us. And this first formation was the harbinger of others to follow. In all 162 bombers in a deadly procession passed all but

A destroyed freighter in its small dry dock.

directly over us, and shortly, from the near distance on the mainland we heard the awful thud of exploding bombs.

This was not to be the last time when, with hearts in our mouths and beating pulses, we watched formations of B-29s flying unmolested over Japan. On one occasion a formation flew directly over the dockyard, and returned on a reciprocal course, convincing us, fortunately incorrectly, that our turn had finally come.

On 28 July our dockyard was again selected as a target and most efficiently attacked by fighter-bombers. Although some two hundred Japanese soldiers and civilians were to be killed in the raid, by some miracle, no prisoners were. Moreover, our camp, which was near enough to the dockyard to be easily mistaken as being associated with it, was also attacked and badly damaged – but although we were told some Japanese who lived in a house across a narrow lane from it were killed, again we had no casualties.

This raid was, as we were to discover later, intended as a prelude to a more serious affair.

By now there were few targets in Japan of major consequence which

Part of Hitachi Dockyard after the attack.

had not been attacked by huge American formations, with devastating effect. One can imagine those whose business it was to plan these raids crossing off the remaining possibilities one by one and pencilling in the dates for destruction of those remaining.

And one of these was Hitachi Dockyard on Innoshima Island – or Habu Dockard, as it was alternatively known.

I have in my possession a reconnaissance photograph of Innoshima Dockyard. In one of those strange coincidences with which life is studded, when I was in Sydney on my way home after the war had ended, I ran across the First Lieutenant off the *Indomitable*, from which we had flown to Java. He told me that it was an aircraft off *Indomitable* which had taken this photograph and that it had been taken during the 28 July attack in which aircraft off *Indomitable* had taken part. And he went on to tell me that a major attack by B-29s on Habu Dockyard had been pencilled in and but for Japan capitulating when she did, would shortly have been carried out. This statement, although I did not know it at the time, was confirmed in Yokohama by American Intelligence to released prisoners from our camp when we were being repatriated and a precise date, 18 August, was given for a B-29 carpet destruction of the Hachi Dock area – a carpet destruction which, no doubt, would have included our camp, which presented a thoroughly military appearance from the air. Had it occurred, far fewer, if any of us, would have left Japan.

Many stories have been put about that careful plans had been laid by the Japanese for the extermination of prisoners when the first Americans landed on Japan itself. I cannot personally vouch for them – but, whether pre-planned or not, I have not the least doubt that this is what would have happened. Had their homeland been invaded the Japanese would have fought like tigers to defend it and they would certainly not have wasted food, time and fighting men to look after inconvenient prisoners. We were, of course, aware of this at the time and found it difficult to reconcile good news with the inevitability which followed from it. As a topic of conversation it was largely avoided; no comforting answer was imaginable. But then no one imagined the atom bomb.

I am entirely satisfied in my own mind that, awful though it was, the atom bomb saved countless lives; lives of the Americans, British and Allied troops who would have attacked Japan, lives of the Japanese who would have defended it. And the lives of the prisoners in Japan, and elsewhere, who, because of their nuisance value and out of the huge groundswell of anger which would have possessed the Japanese nation as their own people were, by the hundreds of thousands, if not by the millions, slaughtered, would not have been allowed to live.

Whether or not this opinion – which is one shared by the great majority of those who were prisoners of the Japanese – is justified, can never be proved. But what in my own case is all but certain, is that one way or another the dropping of the atom bomb a mere twenty-odd miles distant from where we were, which brought about the conclusion of hostilities with a margin of just three days before Habu Dockyard was to be utterly destroyed, gave me my ninth and final life as a fighter pilot and saved the lives of all of those who were with me in Hiroshima 5.

RETURN TO HIROSHIMA

IT had been on a bitterly cold November afternoon that we arrived at the town of Habu on Innoshima Island in the Inland Sea of Japan – one hundred of us, all RAF, and hardly an impressive lot: a shambling group dressed in tropical gear, laden with kitbags, attaché cases, parcels and bundles. Many of us after that voyage of unspeakable horror, were desperately ill and within a few days the first deaths occurred and others followed with depressing regularity.

As one of the hundred RAF I could never forget that first stumbling walk through Habu Dockyard. For sixty-one years I have held in my memory's sight the skeletons of half-built ships, the flash of welding, the smell of burning metal, the faces of the Japanese who watched us go by, the dry docks, the slips, the dumpy travelling cranes. For sixty-one years I have held in my memory's hearing the harsh clang of hammer on metal plate and the woodpecker sound of riveting. For sixty-one years I have remembered the weight of a very sick man I was assisting to stumble along the potholed, unpaved roadway, and the absurdity of wearing a pith helmet in a snowfall.

I helped carry coffins of some of those who died to a crematorium beside the Inland Sea, and of them all, the name I remember best is that of Gibson. Even to remember it now encapsulates the horror of those first dreadful weeks when men died regularly from the illness with which all of us were afflicted. As I lay on the raised platform which was my bed, Gibson's head was separated from mine only by a thin sheet of plywood dividing the rooms in our wooden hut. Through the whole of Boxing Day he alternately screamed or sobbed with the terrible agony of the evil born of that fearful voyage.

Fifty-six years later, I fulfilled a lifetime's ambition. Warmly dressed, escorted by a charming lady sent by the Japanese Foreign Office, welcomed as an honoured lunch guest by an executive of Hitachi-Zosen which owns the dockyard now and owned it then, I walked at my own pace and choice the length and width of that dockyard again. It's changed, of course. They've pulled down a hill to make a huge new dry dock beside the old one I knew so well; there are new machine and plate shops, the dumpy travelling cranes have gone, the roads are paved, and with riveting long-since abandoned and a work-force only one-fifth the size, there is a quieter air. But the flash of welding still sears the eyes, hammers still clang, the smell of burning metal still assaults the nostrils, and the hill behind and the sea in front are quite unchanged. And I could stand again in the places where I had been when Allied aircraft peeled off to strafe and dive-bomb us or where we had stood looking up at *Enola Gay*, which, in a few minutes' time, would drop the bomb which would utterly destroy Hiroshima no more than thirty miles away.

The opportunity of strolling, a free man, through the dockyard where so many cold and hungry precious days of youth were spent obeying the orders of harsh and uncompassionate captors came about in a curious way. I had written *Living With Japanese*, which was based on my experiences as a prisoner of war, and it came to the notice of the National Chairman of the Royal British Legion. I was invited to be a member of a delegation visiting Japan whose members included the Legion's Head of Operations and Development, its Controller of Communications and three Far East prisoners of war.

As the purpose of the visit (defined later in a briefing note) included 'furthering the process of reconciliation between U.K. and Japan', and as it was stated that 'the visit would only be a success if the delegation was seen to be united in its attitudes and comments', I am by no means certain that including three ex-Japanese prisoners of war was the wisest of decisions. No matter how friendly and generous the Japanese might prove to be, locked and irremovable in the minds of ex-prisoners are memories whose effect others, who have not shared so many years of shame and bitterness, cannot truly comprehend.

Be that as it may, the visit was preceded by an invitation to dine with the Japanese Ambassador at his London residence, where I discovered, to my surprise, that the Embassy had purchased several copies of the book and at least partially absorbed its contents.

On our trip to Japan we travelled (and indeed were entertained throughout our visit) Executive Class and on arrival at Narita Airport, Tokyo, were met not only by a representative of the Japanese International Hospitality Conference Association, whose address was given as of the Ministry of Foreign Affairs, but also by quite a clutch of old Japanese gentlemen waving Union Jacks who clustered around us, taking photographs and who, I subsequently discovered, were members of the 'All Burma Veterans Association of Japan', whose representatives were continually to surprise us by appearing in similar clutches to welcome us with flag-waving and camera-flashing at just about every port of call we made. These were men who had known the bitterness of defeat in their long and bloody withdrawal from Imphal when entry into India and victory had seemed almost within their grasp, but there was no question of doubting their pleasure in meeting the delegation. Whenever we arrived at a new destination, there they were waving their Union Jacks and clicking their cameras and presenting us with gifts.

On the second day after arrival we made a pilgrimage to the Commonwealth War Cemetery at Hadogaya and took part in brief services which were concluded by wreath-laying by the National Chairman of the British Legion and other National Council members. I had brought with me a sufficiency of poppies which I was able to place at the foot of the graves of each of those who had died on Innoshima.

Hiroshima was, of course, included in the itinerary and we arrived by bullet train a day earlier than originally planned as a heavy snow-fall in Hakone (to which we had driven by coach after Hadogaya) threatened to maroon the delegation if socks were not rapidly pulled up. Indeed they were, and so effectively that when we arrived at the station nearly twenty-four hours earlier than expected, there, to greet us with their flags and cameras, after only an hour or two of notice, were more members of the All Burma Veterans Association.

A visit to Hiroshima is an unforgettable experience. Here is a town which until the atom bomb was dropped had not been attacked by Allied aircraft and which contains as a relic of its earlier existence only

Wreath-laying ceremony at the Hiroshima Peace Memorial Cenotaph. Author front row, second from left.

the remains of a single building – the one-time Prefectural Exhibition Hall: a three-storied, partly steel-framed brick structure with a five-storied tower with a domed roof. It is an awe-inspiring thing to gaze from a twentieth floor at a modern, well laid out city with its buildings, rivers, roads and parks and visualise the approach across the Inland Sea of a single aircraft which contains within its belly the power to destroy utterly with a single bomb a town of such consequence.

There is a Peace Memorial Museum dedicated to the 'abolition of nuclear weapons and the realization of lasting peace'. This Museum must leave in the minds of all who walk through its halls an unforgettable apprehension of the scale of the awfulness wrought on that August morning. Amongst the innumerable, often horrifying, exhibits there are two reconstructions of the city which once existed. The first shows Hiroshima as it was before the atom bomb exploded 580 metres above the town; the second, as it was a few seconds later. These models are very large, the first indicating every house and building – the houses small, single-storied, huddling close together around narrow lanes with, in the entire town, only about half a dozen two- or three-storied buildings. In the second reconstruction there are literally no small houses left; all are reduced to dust and the few major buildings are gutted shells. Around these reconstructions are panels on which the story is told:

> That morning began like any other morning with people hurrying to work. 8.15 a.m. August 6th, 1945, Hiroshima was a picturesque quiet city. Then with a blinding flash and a deafening roar a single bomb burned it to the ground. An entire city was instantaneously destroyed beyond recognition. Nearly all people and buildings within a two kilometre radius of the hypo-centre were killed or destroyed. By the end of the year approximately 140,000 were dead or missing – nearly half of the almost 315,000 residents. Hiroshima was a charred plain as far as the eye could see. Survivors claimed they could stand at Hiroshima station and see Ujina Port. Those who entered the city out of concern for their relatives or to help with relief efforts were exposed to residual radiation. Tremendous numbers of unidentifiable corpses were piled up and cremated on the spot. The injured and irradiated continued to die. Day and night in every corner of the city corpses were piled upon corpses and burnt.

The survivors called the atom bomb *'Pika Don'*. *Pika* referred to the flash of light; *Don* was the onomatopœic reference to the tremendous sound.

The Hiroshima Peace Memorial Cenotaph, as it is called, at which the delegation held its second wreath-laying ceremony, is the simplest of structures, consisting of an extended arch, elliptical in section. It is very close to the hypo-centre of the A-bomb and through it one can see the 'A-bomb Dome' – as the remains of the surviving relic of pre-bomb Hiroshima are called. A little to the side of the imaginary line which joins the two is the 'A-bomb Children's Structure'. This is a simple monument capped by the figure of a child and is always drenched at its base with a great mass of multi-coloured paper. It seems that a girl dying from radiation sickness took to making paper cranes (birds) out of the wrappings in which her medicine was delivered, and that from this a cult has grown, and paper cranes threaded on string in a myriad of colours are placed by individuals as offerings for peace.

After Hiroshima we went to Kyoto, which I had always imagined to be a place of such religious significance as to be entirely separated from the essential secularism of Japan's commercial towns – as, no doubt, not all that many years ago it was. But now Osaka has spread so brutally as, in effect, to reach almost to the very margins of the temple area. Here a little of the old Japan remains in narrow streets lined with attractive houses with gables, balconies and complicated pantiled roofs, now, of course, largely converted into tourist shops, but none the less delightful and curiously reassuring.

In the car park to the temple complex who should be awaiting us but the eager representatives of the All Burma Veterans Association carrying, as well as their small flags, a full-blown Union Jack. After the usual greetings and camera-clicking we progressed through a formal archway where we were handed purple joss sticks which we were required to deposit, still burning, in a roofed iron receptacle filled with sand, before following a black-robed priest into the outer chamber of the shrine, within which are memorial tablets to two million Japanese who died in the war. Behind the building there is a huge concrete Buddha unveiled in 1955 'in commemoration of those Japanese who sacrificed themselves in the last war and for the establishment of a peaceful Japan'. Beyond the Buddha there is a Memorial Hall in which there is a sculpture of a lightly draped lady on a stand beside a large stone tablet on which is inscribed a poem to world peace and universal brotherhood. Below is the obligatory casket containing the ashes of an unknown soldier 'erected to the memory of more than forty-eight thousand foreign soldiers who perished on Japanese territory or on territory under Japanese military control.'

Close by in a small building is a cabinet containing upwards of fifty drawers in which are stored the names of American, Australian,

British, Canadian, Dutch, New Zealand and other nationals who 'perished in territory under Japanese jurisdiction', and it was a simple matter for me to find the card of a close friend who had died on Innoshima: 'Lee John, S L/Cpl. 4667546 1/10/44 Acute pneumonia. Cremated Myotikuji, Mitsonoshio-achi, Hiroshima-Ken, Japan.'

And so I had come, as it were, full circle. I had been to the island where John Stirling Lee and the others had died, I had paid my respects at their graves at Hadogaya and now I had found the record of their deaths safely filed away in Kyoto. Above all I had been back to Hiroshima-Ken to the place where, in one split second of awfulness, the bomb which was to change the pattern of thought in our world for ever had exploded – the bomb which, in killing 140,000 men and women in a peaceful and picturesque town, had unquestionably saved the lives of millions – including those of the surviving Japanese prisoners of war, who would never have come home had it not been dropped.

Through ten days I had perhaps come as close to living with Japanese as is possible for a visitor to a foreign country. Throughout the stay I had met with nothing but courtesy, generosity, kindness, good-humour, consideration and so far as we, their one-time enemies were concerned, forgiveness. The mission was intended to further the process of reconciliation and I have no doubt that insofar as most members of the delegation were concerned it went some way to achieving that object. But for myself? Well, it is difficult. I have no doubt that most of the Japanese I met genuinely wished to put the past behind them, in most cases had long since done so. But for one who has been a Japanese prisoner of war it is not so simple.

INDEX

The index is arranged alphabetically except for entries under the author's name, which are in chronological order. Page numbers in *italics* refer to illustrations.